THOSE WHO PONDER PROVERBS:
APHORISTIC THINKING AND
BIBLICAL LITERATURE

JAMES G. WILLIAMS

BIBLE AND LITERATURE
SERIES

Editor
David M. Gunn

THOSE WHO PONDER PROVERBS

Aphoristic Thinking
and Biblical Literature

JAMES G. WILLIAMS

1981

SHEFFIELD

THE ALMOND PRESS

BIBLE AND LITERATURE SERIES, 2

Copyright © 1981 The Almond Press

British Library Cataloguing in Publication Data:

Williams, James G
    Those who ponder proverbs: aphoristic thinking
    and Biblical literature. - (Bible and literature
    series, ISSN 0260-4493;2)
    I. Title   II. Series
    220   BS511.2

    ISBN 0-907459-02-1
    ISBN 0-907459-03-X Pbk

Published by
The Almond Press
P.O. Box 208
Sheffield S10 5DW
England

The typescript for this book was input to a word
processor by Altertext, Inc., Boston, through an
omni-font scanner. No special preparation to the
typescript was made.

Printed in Great Britain
by Redwood Burn Limited
Trowbridge & Esher
1981

FOR YVONNE

CONTENTS

ACKNOWLEDGMENTS

It is a great pleasure to acknowledge the help and encouragement that I have received. Syracuse University granted me a subvented research leave for the spring semester of 1980, and the erstwhile chairman of the Department of Religion, Associate Dean Ronald Cavanagh, supported me strongly in this and other projects.

Some of the ideas and materials in this book were first presented in a lecture to biblical students and professors in the Faculté de Théologie Catholique de l'Université des Sciences Humaines de Strasbourg. I hold warm memories of the cordial reception given me by Dean B. Renaud and his colleagues Kuntzmann, Schlosser, and Join-Lambert, and I thank my good friend Georges Henry of Strasbourg for working with me to set my French "anglais" in French "français."

Professor Gerhard Neumann gave freely of his time in four days of stimulating discussion on aphoristic and narrative discourse in Freiburg im Breisgau. Professors Sheldon Blank of Hebrew Union College - Jewish Institute of Religion and William Beardslee of Emory University made valuable comments on the work in progress. A. Leland Jamison, professor emeritus of New Testament, has been a constant friend and biblical Gesprächpartner. My graduate assistant, Joyce Mauber, has assisted me ably in typing and indexing.

To Donald Morton, professor of English literature at Syracuse University, I owe a great debt: he has taught me much about aphoristic discourse, and his critique of an earlier draft helped me to see what I intended to say and how I would say it.

Finally and first of all, I dedicate this work to Yvonne, in whom her husband's heart has trust.

Syracuse, New York
Advent, 1980

PERIODICAL ABBREVIATIONS

DVjs	Deutsche Vierteljahrschrift für Literaturwissenschaft und Geistesgeschichte
HUCA	Hebrew Union College Annual
JAAR	Journal of the American Academy of Religion
JBL	Journal of Biblical Literature
MLR	Modern Language Review
PMLA	Proceedings of the Modern Language Association
ZAW	Zeitschrift für die alttestamentliche Wissenschaft

PREFACE

Who digs a pit will fall in it,
Who rolls a stone, it will roll back on him.
                        (Prov 26:27)

Who digs no grave for another falls in it
himself.
                        (Karl Kraus)[1]

The mind of the intelligent man will ponder a
parable....
                        (Sirach 3:29a)[2]

Biblical wisdom is characteristically cast in "short
forms" - in aphoristic discourse. Although there
are problems in clarifying what "aphorism" is and
what it does, it is clear that aphoristic or
"gnomic" utterance is an important part of
biblical literature and thought. Moreover, many poets and
thinkers in modern western culture have attached great
importance to the aphoristic mode of discourse, however it
may be defined. Pascal claimed that his "disordered"
articulation of thoughts was the only way to intimate the
"true order" in a fallen world (Pensée 532).[3] Lichtenberg
preferred the brief statement of thoughts (Gedanken) rather
than the development of a philosophical system, for a
system, he asserted, seduces one into preceding perception
rather than following it (Sudelbücher D 485).[4] Kafka
devoted much of his concern and energy to the composition
of aphorisms and parables. The aphoristic mode has also
been important for other authors and thinkers, such as Oscar
Wilde, Friedrich Nietzsche, Jean Paul, Karl Kraus, Paul
Valéry, and Stanislaw Lec. A deliberately aphoristic style
informs the work of Martin Buber (I and Thou), Abraham

Heschel (God in Search of Man, inter alia), and Norman O. Brown (Love's Body). As William Beardslee has put it,

> In our modern situation, the aphoristic or proverbial form ... is felt to be appropriate both as an expression of the fragmentariness of existence and of the possibility of imposing a human vision on existence in spite of its fragmentariness.[5]

The conviction that any truth to be found in human existence is to be discovered in manifold actualities or fragments is not rare in modern thought, and one often encounters the desire to construct various "occasions" of order rather than a total system. These two factors are undoubtedly important in accounting for modern interest in aphoristic language. Yet short, non-narrative forms are an ancient human product, so the modern interest in aphorism is by no means a new phenomenon. Furthermore, the usual reasons given for its modern importance often fail to take note of its distinctiveness and complexities. If aphoristic discourse functions as an antidiscursive mode of expression, it is not perforce antiphilosophical. If it is frequently employed to disorient and to undercut conventional uses of language, it is still often an experiment in forming a new and vital language.

It will be the thesis of this study that the only way adequately to understand the function of aphoristic language in the sources to be investigated is to view it as both literary and conceptual, both poetic and philosophical. The argument, it is hoped, will contribute modestly to the use of literary criticism in religious studies. However, the primary and specific objective of the essay is to illumine the biblical texts usually considered "aphoristic," namely those wisdom writings and other sources where short, non-narrative forms are the mode of expression. Were the Hebrew "māšāl" and the Greek "parabolē" special vehicles for a certain kind of aesthetic and cognitive response to experience? Did they presuppose and transmit a kind of consciousness and perspective that could not be exactly communicated in other ways? Is there a generic relationship between the traditional proverb transmitted in an ancient, conservative society and the aphorism of the modern writer whose thinking is informed by the relativity of knowledge and the tenuousness of language?

Preface

There are biblical interpreters of the recent past who have addressed themselves to aspects of these questions. This study will not seek to review their work, but our indebtedness to them will be obvious, as indicated in the reference notes. Of seminal influence on this writer have been Gerhard von Rad and William A. Beardslee. Von Rad's handling of both literary and phenomenological aspects of gnomic wisdom is, in our opinion, highly informative. Beardslee has combined literary studies of gnomic discourse with a process theological perspective that may become an enriching conceptuality in biblical hermeneutics.

However, no one has so far undertaken an extensive study that draws upon the resources of contemporary literary criticism in probing both the aesthetic and cognitive sides of gnomic forms. This we propose to do in this little work. The reader may well have questions about certain matters which will not be treated in the text of this study. A word is therefore in order about terminology, the criteria by which biblical sources were selected for treatment and critical presuppositions concerning the biblical sources.

(1) Terminology

The writer considered it unprofitable to give an initial definition of "aphorism," "proverb," and other terms such as "gnome," "maxim," "sentence," etc. The reasons for not doing so will be given in Chapter IV (see IV. B. (1), "Problem of Definition" and the excursus, "Aphorism and Proverb"). Phrases such as "aphoristic discourse" and "gnomic discourse" will be used interchangeably. Their meaning will doubtless be clear to the reader long before we focus on the problem of definition in the last chapter.

(2) Criteria for Selecting Biblical Works

The primary biblical sources for this study are Proverbs, Ecclesiastes (Kohelet), Ecclesiasticus (Sirach), and the gospels of Matthew, Mark, and Luke. Occasional reference will also be made to the Talmudic tractate Abot, since the ancient Jewish wisdom tradition made such an obvious contribution to its form and content. Proverbs, Kohelet and Sirach were selected as definitely "aphoristic," i.e., they are made up of relatively short and isolable nonnarrative forms that do not seek to sum up a set of beliefs or systematize a point of view, but look at man, God, world, and society from a number of angles. The book of Job will be mentioned a few times, but it is not one of our main sources because the proverbial forms therein, though many, serve a primarily rhetorical function; they are not the chief mode of expression in their own right. The book of Wisdom (or Wisdom of Solomon) was not chosen for similar reasons: the binary "māšāl" (proverb) is employed, but it is subsumed under a sustained doctrinal discourse.[6]

As for the synoptic gospels, they are of course not wisdom books, but they present many sayings of Jesus, and the gospels of Matthew and Luke have large collections of teachings. Their aphoristic wisdom content is so important that it was decided to include the parabolic sayings of Jesus in this study. Any list of the gnomic material in the gospels will attest that Jesus was known as a teacher of aphoristic wisdom.[7]

(3) Critical Presuppositions

There will be little in this study pertaining to dating and the establishment of historical and social context. By and large common opinions and hypotheses, expressing a consensus in biblical criticism, will be accepted. For example, we shall assume that the collections of Prov 10-22:16 and 25-29 probably represent an older, preexilic stage of the wisdom tradition, that 22:17-24:22 may be later, perhaps exilic, and that Prov 1-9 is postexilic in its present form. As for the book of Job, it shall be considered postexilic.[8]

Concerning the aphoristic wisdom of Jesus, an attempt has been made to draw upon Q material as much as possible.[9] This does not, however, guarantee "authenticity." There is no reason why non-Q sayings could not also be the teachings of Jesus or represent the early church's understanding of how and what Jesus taught.

There is one dominant doctrine in modern New Testament criticism with which we disagree strongly. This is the so-called "criterion of dissimilarity" as it has been used by Bultmann and some of his heirs in biblical interpretation and hermeneutics. Our reasons for disagreement will be stated in an excursus in Chapter III.

To conclude this preface, the author can think of nothing better than to quote Karl Kraus's aphorism:[10]

> The thought comes because I take it
> with the word.

Chapter I

ANCIENT APHORISTIC WISDOM OF THE JEWS:
FOUR MOTIFS

F basic motifs constituting the aphoristic wisdom of the biblical period none are more important than these four: retribution and divine justice, wise utterance, tradition and the fathers, and individual self-discipline. Distinct yet interrelated, they are the motifs that make up the dynamics of traditional wisdom.[1] There is now a consensus in biblical studies that a concept of order is at the very center of wisdom thinking, and this concept of order is usually linked to an understanding of divine rule and divine justice.[2] The order of things manifests itself in a retributive principle of justice. This order is, in turn, mediated in human existence through the proper use of language. Speech is a capacity which carries the power to make order known or threaten it, to seal human relations or undercut them, to deal in life or death, so to say (see Prov 18:21). This quest for order as centered and represented in right speech requires an ordering of the self, a self-control entailing restraint of one's emotions and appetites. The ordering of the self also requires the recognition and maintenance of the agents of authority through which one is guided and formed to be wise in speech and conduct and to have confidence in the order of things. These agents are supremely the "fathers" who transmit the wisdom tradition.

A discussion of these motifs will establish a point of departure and reference for the present study, whose objective is to examine the relation of aphoristic discourse in biblical literature to kinds of consciousness and knowledge. We shall investigate the ways in which gnomic forms express perspectives on existence in the world, and how these perspectives are related to the forms of expression. This objective requires a survey of the essentials of wisdom thinking, its very bases, which the author identifies as the motifs indicated above. Three of these, retribution and justice, wise utterance, and tradition and the fathers, appear repeatedly in the scholarly literature. Less attention has been devoted to self-control, though some recent studies have shed new light on its importance.[3] Although aphoristic wisdom encompasses a great many concerns and topics, these motifs have emerged in the author's research as crucial in the consideration of the kind of consciousness and knowledge that gnomic forms in the Bible presuppose and express.

A. Order: Retribution and Divine Justice

As one orients oneself to the world and gives to it, so one receives from it. The world - the totality of social and natural reality that environs man - is retributive (cf. Latin "retribuare," to pay, grant, repay).

Of no profit are treasures of wickedness,
and righteousness delivers from death.
(Prov 10:2)

The solemn truth![4] The evil man won't be acquitted,
and the children of the righteous will go free.
(Prov 11:21)

This retributive principle is sometimes referred to the governance of Yahweh:

Yahweh does not allow the soul of the righteous to starve,
and the desire of the wicked he obstructs.
(Prov 10:3)

These are typical cases: usually or typically one obtains results in terms of what one gives and how one takes a stance toward others. A kind of piously humble attempt to harmonize one's life with the order of things brings success, prosperity, tranquility.

On the other hand, biblical wisdom does not express the notion of retribution in a strict causal sense. While it is not correct to deny a doctrine of retribution in the wisdom tradition,[5] it is also not true that there is a systematic doctrine of retribution that asserts precise causal connections. For one thing, the very language of the "sentence" proverbs[6] is far removed from formal concepts of causality. Connections are made, rather, through juxtaposition:

> Who restrains his words has knowledge,
> and who keeps his temper is a discerning man.
>
> (Prov 17:27)

Here two observations are juxtaposed to each other. We learn that there a relation of "restraint" and "knowledge," but it would go too far to say that one causes or produces the other. And even in an "instruction"[7] proverb which has a causal conjuction ("kî": "for" or "because"), the very form often amounts to a placing together of assertions. For instance:

> Speak not in the ears of the senseless,
> for he will refuse the wisdom of your words.
>
> (Prov 23:9)

This is practically the same as being informed

> Speak not in the ears of the senseless.
> The senseless will refuse the sense of your words.

One finds out why wisdom is refused, namely that the fool cannot assimilate wise words. But one does not learn that "senselessness" is caused in a strict sense, or that one should never speak to the foolish person because the result will always be the same (see Prov 26:4-5). Such conclusions move beyond the range and intention of these proverbs. Indeed, the assertion, for example, "Whoever trusts in wealth will fall," could be called cause and effect thinking in one sense (Y is typically the result of X). But this is not a strict and hard determinism that holds "all X leads to Y" and "Y is always the result of X". This mental movement is practically never made in the wisdom tradition.[8] Furthermore, the aphoristic style of thinking in most of the literature precludes an abstract, systematic doctrine of causation. This will be discussed in Chapter II.

On the other hand, there is a definite relation of deeds and consequences, as already indicated. Such and such an attitude and pattern of behavior results typically (not always, not necessarily) in such and such an outcome - this is the retributive principle of comportment.

> Whoever keeps his mouth and tongue
> keeps his life from troubles.
>
> (Prov 21:23)
>
> Before man are life and death,
> whichever he chooses will be given him.
>
> (Sir 15:17)
>
> Rabbi Yehoshua said: The evil eye and the evil principle
> and hatred of fellow creatures expel one from the world.
>
> (Abot 2:16)

This quest to affirm and express the order of things in the form of retributive justice did not go unquestioned. Job, in the anguish of his suffering, denied the retributive principle (Job 21:17-21). Kohelet engaged in a sustained argument against the doctrine of retributive justice.[9] There is no justice for the oppressed (Koh 4:1), human existence is "vapor"[10] like all things and events in the world (Koh 1:2, passim), and there is no profit or lasting value to gain in the world (Koh 1:3; 2:11; passim). There is only a "portion," joy and satisfaction in certain experiences, that one can receive.[11]

In the proverbs and parables of Jesus we find a protest against the principle of retribution, in the sense that he opposed the ancient wisdom conviction "that the workings of man's social interrelationship would bring about a reward for righteousness in this world."[12] He did affirm the justice of God in an imminent final judgment (Matt 7:1-2), but it would reverse traditional expectations; the humble would be exalted and the exalted humbled (Matt 23:12; Lk 14:11; passim). This ultimate order would be reached only by dying to the present order:

> For whoever would save his life will lose it; and
> whoever saves his life for my sake and the gospel's will
> find it.
>
> (Mk 8:35)

We find in these protests against the principle of retribution a combination of experience and expression set in opposition to the received tradition. Job experienced extreme loss and suffering though he had been accounted righteous, and he receives in the end a new vision of God and creation.[13] Kohelet agonizes over the fact of

mortality and recommends a partial antidote in the realm of
immediate feelings and relations. Jesus concerns himself
with human care and anxiety and announces an arriving
realm of God, the good Father (Matt 6:25-34; Luke 12:22-31).
Yet all of these protesters are concerned with traditional
notions of retribution and divine justice even as they
counter them with their own teachings.[14]

The concept of order that is expressed in retributive
justice has its focus in language. It is through speaking that
relationships are established and the world is revealed.
Although quantitative evidence is not decisive, it is
nonetheless interesting and relevant that the Hebrew words
"lāšôn" ("tongue, speech, language") and "peh" ("mouth")
occur with a frequency disproportionate to the size of the
book of Proverbs (the former 19 times, the latter 52
times).[15]

> Free yourself of a perverse mouth,
> and devious words put far from you.
>
> (Prov 4:24)
>
> A source of life is the mouth of the righteous,
> and the wicked man's mouth conceals violence.
>
> (Prov 10:11)
>
> Legs handing from the lame
> and a proverb in the mouth of fools.
>
> (Prov 26:7)
>
> Deep waters are the words of a man's mouth....
>
> (Prov 18.4)

See also in Sirach:

> O that a guard were set over my mouth,
> and a seal of prudence upon my lips,
> that it might keep me from falling,
> so that my tongue might not destroy me!
>
> (Sir 22:27)

These examples show that confidence in the proper use of
language and the principle of retribution are interrelated. It
is therefore no accident that Kohelet's loss of faith in a
knowable moral order is coterminous with a loss of
confidence in the adequacy of language. Human speech
cannot utter the wearisome cycle of things (Koh 1:8), and
words of wise counsel are often ineffective (Koh 9:16-18).
Primitive Christianity, although affirming an eschatological

principle of justice, attributed to Jesus many statements showing a distrust of the ordinary uses of language which went far beyond the traditional Jewish caution and restraint in speech. Believers are not to swear any oath at all, but to say only yes or no (Matt 5:33-37). A distance, indeed a dichotomy, is posited between verbal expression of faith and actual faith:

> Not everyone who says to me, "Lord, Lord," shall enter the kingdom of heaven, but he who does the will of my Father who is in heaven.
>
> (Matt 7:21)

The just order of things is thus one in which language functions in a stable correspondence to the way things are. But the order informed by retribution is such that human existence is often experienced as paradoxical. Man's thoughts, schemes and words are not finally under his control (Prov 16:1, 9; 19:21; 20:24; 21:30-31; 26:27). Even if the world is completely orderly, it is nonetheless ultimately a maze from the human point of view; whether ultimately from the world order or from Yahweh, one's destiny is not one's own. Retribution is thus a two-edged sword: it asserts that life makes sense because there is a connection of thinking - doing - result, but one's thinking and doing are limited by a transcendent justice that may bring one's thinking and doing to unforeseen and ironic results. The doctrine of retributive justice is a bridge of thought and language between consciousness and environing reality, social and cosmic. But the bridge may collapse, or to change the image, the road may go where one did not expect.

> To man are the mind's preparations,
> and from Yahweh is the tongue's response.
>
> (Prov 16:1)

> Man's mind minds his way,
> and Yahweh steers his step.
>
> (Prov 16:9)

Jesus also affirms this mystery of man's unforeseen end, although he transforms it into the context of faith in the transcendent justice of God that will be fully realized in the new age.

> So the last will be first and the first last.
>
> (Matt 20:16/Mk 10:31/Lk 13.30)

22

But in spite of the fact that the human mind cannot finally comprehend the way of the world and the way of God, the wisdom tradition expressed a great confidence in the dependability and bounty of the world; and the aphoristic wisdom that is theological views God as good and just. Yahweh oversees human life (Prov 16:1-9), he concerns himself with justice (Prov 16:11), he is the redeemer (gōʼēl) of the poor (Prov 22:22-23; 23:10-11).[16] Yahweh is an impartial judge, "ʼᵉlōhê mišpāṭ," "God of justice," who heeds the supplications of the widow and orphan (Sir 35:12-14). According to the gospels, Jesus taught that the God of Israel is a Father who will care for the individual just as he feeds the birds and clothes the grass (Matt 6:26, 30/Lk 12:24, 28). God will respond to humans by analogy with a good father providing for his children (Matt 7:9-11/Lk 11:11-13).

Sirach is the one work in the aphoristic tradition which attempts a conceptually sustained and rhetorically wrought theodicy. He seeks to counter skepticism in Jewish circles that emerges in the hellenistic period,[17] and he utilizes not only a debate form[18] but he bases his theological case on a principle of oppositions in creation (33:7-15; 42:24-25).

> Good is the opposite of evil,
> and life is the opposite of death;
> so the sinner is the opposite of the godly.
> Look upon all the works of the Most High:
> they likewise are pairs, one the opposite of the other.
>
> (33:14-15)

This principle of oppositions corresponds to Sirach's rhetorical style (see Chapter II, 37). Although it is employed to declare the divine justice and goodness, it brings a certain ambiguity into the theodicy. All the deeds of God are good "in their time" (Sir 39:30-33), but in the wrong time they may be experienced as evil. With this concept Sirach concedes that "from man's point of view, the divine rule can be evaluated as completely negative...."[19] Nevertheless, God is just, good and powerful beyond all human understanding.

> To the end we cannot attain,
> and this is the final word: He is the all.
>
> (Sir 43:27)

B. Language: Wise Utterance

The capacity to think, to put thoughts into words and words into thoughts, is power; it is the possibility of creating ideas and symbols that constitute a human world. It is the possibility of establishing good and evil situations in the world.

Death and life are in the power of language,
and her lovers will eat of her fruit.

(Prov 18:21)

Words can damage, but they can also heal:

A gentle tongue removes wrath,
but a harsh word stirs up anger.

(Prov 15:1)

A healing tongue is a tree of life,
but perverseness therein is a wound in the spirit.

(Prov 15:4)

One of the few real literary paradoxes in Proverbs captures the effectiveness of the patient, wise counsel:

With patience is a ruler persuaded,
and a gentle tongue breaks bone.

(Prov 25:15)

In testimony the person who is honest and who sides with the righteous will be blessed (Prov 24:24-25).

Whoever gives a truthful answer kisses the lips.

(Prov 24:26)

Language, in the large sense of thinking, speaking and counseling, is at the very depth of the human reality:

The words of the mouth are deep waters,
a rushing torrent is the source of wisdom.[20]

(Prov 18:4)

Counsel is like deep water in a man's heart,
but the man of understanding will draw it out.

(Prov 20:5)

Given this creative and destructive potential of language, it is necessary to watch one's words, to listen, to understand and regulate one's life:

The mouth of the fool is his ruin,

and his lips the snare of his life.

(Prov 18:7)

...whoever multiples words occasions sin.

(Abot 1:17)

But the wise word, which is always a timely word, is an occasion of joy:

A person gets pleasure from an apt reply,
and how salutary is a word in season![21]

(Prov 15:23)

This concern with the proper understanding and use of language moves thus into the area of self-discipline, which will be taken up below.

The theme of language is so pervasive in older wisdom, as represented in Proverbs, that it may even be the key to comprehending the image of the "stranger woman" who appears as a seductive lure to the man trying to negotiate his way through life's hazards. S. Amsler has shown[22] that her weapons are not so much her beauty or sexually seductive wiles as her manner of using language. It is her "coaxing words" (Prov 2:16; 6:24; 7:5, 21), her lips that drop honeyed words (5:3), her "flattering speech" (7:21), her mouth like a deep pit (22:14), that hold the power of entrapment. "It is by her word (parole) that the stranger woman exercises her power of fascination over the man."[23]

Sirach follows in the ancient wisdom tradition in his appreciation of the power of language, and he concentrates quite deliberately on the proverb. The wise man, above all the "scribe" (Heb. sōp̄ēr), who is the sage par excellence, will ponder proverbs and compose them. The scribe

will preserve the sayings of notable men,
and pentrate the subtleties of parables;
he will seek out the hidden meanings of proverbs,
and be at home with the obscurities of parables.

(Sir 39:2-3)

The intelligent man will "discern the proverbs of the wise" (Sir 3:27).[24] Indeed,

Those who understand sayings become wise themselves
and pour forth apt proverbs.

(Sir 18:29)

Kohelet and Jesus both presuppose the importance of

Those Who Ponder Proverbs

language and use striking images, but they attempt to
undermine a traditional use of language by disorienting the
audience. Kohelet's primary strategy of disorientation is to
utilize contrasting proverbs in order to contradict
traditional wisdom and leave a sense of distrust of the
capacity of wisdom to represent reality. This strategy will
be discussed in Chapter III, but here is one example:

A good name is better than fine perfume[25]
and the day of death than the day of birth.

(Koh 7:1)

The second stich is not only contrary to the Jewish tradition
of the value of life, it reads like a Zen "koan" after the
traditional thought of the first line.

As for Jesus, he was known as a master of language, using
an abundance of metaphors that were memorable to the
earliest followers. He was a speaker in parables (Mk 4:33-34;
Matt 13:34-35). His teachings were often paradoxical, and
there is a strong tradition that his parables were difficult to
comprehend (Mk 4:10-12; Matt 13:10-13; Lk 8:9-10). Many
sayings are expressions of the paradox that one must "die"
or "lose" in order to "live":

...whoever loses his life will preserve it"

(Lk 17:33)

Blessed are you, when men hate you....

(Lk 6:22)

He who humbles himself will be exalted.

(Lk 14:11)

The paradoxical proverbs "aim to interrupt the flow of the
moments of life in continuous connection to break the vision
that orients this flow."[26] Paul Ricoeur has called this the
strategy of "reorientation by disorientation."[27]

C. Authority: Tradition and the Fathers

We know from the wisdom books of the Hebrew Scriptures
and the Apocrypha that a definite tradition of the "fathers"
had emerged by some period in ancient Israelite wisdom,
probably no later than the postexilic epoch (Job 8:8-10;
15:17-19; 20:4-5; Sir 2:10; 8:9; Prov 1:5; 8 and passim; 22:17).
Von Rad has said that the sentence proverbs originated in
experience, and that if

a sentence originated from the experience of the fathers, then it could already of itself claim for itself normative significance.[28]

Von Rad's statement needs to be qualified somewhat if applied to the entirety of the book of Proverbs, as the two collections attributed to Solomon, 10:1 - 22:16 and 25-29, do not explicitly present the symbol of the "fathers" as the embodiment of the tradition. Still, the father as a role-type (parent, teacher) is important in the presumably older Solomonic collections, and we clearly see in Proverbs the idea of an ancient collective voice that speaks to the son in the present.[29]

Hear, my son, the instruction of your father,
and forsake not the teaching of your mother.
(Prov 1:8)

My son, fear Yahweh and the king;
with innovators[30] do not involve yourself.
(24:21)

Despise not to hear the aged
who heard from their fathers[31]....
(Sir 8:9; see 8:8)

The wisdom of the fathers as embodying and representing the tradition was taken up directly in the Talmudic tractate "Abot" ("Fathers") whose contents are a collection of the sayings and maxims of the sages of the twofold Torah, the written and the oral.

The authority of the "voice" uttering the aphoristic wisdom of the fathers is that of a human subject, but it is not the authority of the individual. Even though all proverbs must originate with or be composed by some person,[32] and though many were doubtless fresh and full of insight in their own time, their intention is not to set the individual speaker in the forefront. They are often deliberately archaizing. A. J. Greimas has said, "The archaic character of proverbs constitutes ... a placement outside of time of their meanings."[33] They express "the wisdom of all the ancients" (sophian pantōn archaiōn, Sir 39:1).

Kohelet breaks away from the authority of the ancient collective voice. For him the limited wisdom that human beings can attain is drawn from the experience of the individual. He holds that there is a type of person who is a "fool," and there is a "wisdom," a very practical wisdom that can be found. But Kohelet's thinking and literary style give center stage to the voice of the individual self. Michael Fox has described this voice as that of the experiencing "I" as represented by the narrating "I."[34] The "royal fiction" that follows the prologue, which may be limited to 1:12-2:11,[35] is a good indication of the self that searches out experience for what wisdom can be found.

> And I applied my mind to seek and explore by wisdom concerning all that is done under heaven....
>
> (Koh 1:13)
>
> Then I said to myself, "Come let me try out in joy, and enjoy pleasure."
>
> (Koh 2:1)

Over and over again Kohelet speaks in the first person of his experience and knowledge: I know, I have seen, I have considered, etc. In keeping with his denial of the traditional concepts of retributive justice and the power and adequacy of language, his authority is that of the voice of individual experience.[36]

Jesus speaks often in the first person, and frequently his authority is emphasized: "You have heard that it was said[37] ... but I say unto you" (Matt 5:21-22, 27-28, 31-32, 33-34, 38-39, 43-44). The authority of the teachings of Jesus becomes even more complex when the proverbial wisdom teachings and quotations of ancient sayings are examined (e.g., Matt 11:19b/Lk 7:35; Matt 24:28/Lk 17:37; Mk 6:4 pars.; Matt 10:16/Lk 11:3). For example in Matt 11:7-19/Lk 7:24-35 the authority of the speaker is grounded in an ancient collective wisdom ("yet wisdom is justified by her deeds," Matt 11:19b; "all her children" in Luke). Yet the speaker refers to the "son of man" (Matt 11:19a/Lk 7:34), which designates Jesus himself in this context. Whether the title is here an instance of the polite first person reference[38] or indicates the eschatological identity of Jesus (the evangelists' understanding), the speaker is clearly a herald of God's reign. The early church and the evangelists believed the voice of Jesus to be God's own voice. Thus the portrait of Jesus in the synoptic gospels is that of a human voice citing ancient human wisdom, yet the voice speaks God's own word while calling the wisdom tradition into question.

D. The Individual: Discipline and Self-Control

The aphoristic forms of traditional wisdom are bearers of order in their balance of "parallelismus membrorum," and the content thereof was frequently concerned with little pictures of order. The ancient Jewish proverbs characteristically advocate, whether by implication through observation or explicitly by instruction, a life of disciplined self-control. There is no systematic view of the human self, but the self is seen as ideally a multi-faceted order that is kept in check by wisdom.

> A wise man is cautious in everything,
> and in days of sin he guards against wrongdoing.
>> (Sir 18:27)
>
> Do you follow your base desires,
> but restrain your appetites.
>> (Sir 18:30)

Images of the "hot" and "cold" person are especially revealing with respect to the motif of self-control, for the words for temperature become metaphors of license and restraint. It is the "cold" person who is approved and recommended.

> The irascible man ('îš ḥēmâ, "man of heat")
>   provokes quarrels,
> the patient man settles strife.
>> (Prov 15:18)
>
> Who restrains his words has knowledge,
> and who keeps his temper (qar rûaḥ, "cold of spirit")
> is a discerning man.
>> (Prov 17:27; see Abot 1:17)

Instructive also are the images of passion and seduction in the less compact short forms of Prov 1-9. For example, the "fire" that can consume one's life, namely sexual passion:

> Can a man hide fire in his heart
> without setting his clothes aflame?
> Or can one march upon coals
> without burning one's feet?
>> (Prov 6:27-28)

The context of these verses is an exhortation to lead the disciplined life. In the disciplined life one must face two "fires" or passions: the one is the desire for the instruction of the parents and elders, the other is the destructive passion for a woman. "...The sages must master themselves in order to kindle the one and extinguish the other."[39] The only two pleasures deriving from deep desire that are recommended to the adult male are those of the husband with his wife (Prov 5:18-19) and the sage with wisdom.

Whoever keeps the law controls his thoughts,
and wisdom is the fulfilment of the law of the Lord.
(Sir 21:11)

L. L. Thompson has suggested that Mary Douglas's concept of correlation "between a constrained social system and bodily control seems to hold in Proverbs."[40] Thompson notes the frequency of images of keeping and guarding one's language and behavior:

Keep them [words of the father]
in the midst of your heart.

(Prov 4:21)

Whoever keeps his mouth and tongue
keeps his life from troubles.

(Prov 21:23)

The primary objective of the individual is therefore to be disciplined in order to control himself and guard traditional wisdom; he will thereby help maintain the tradition and social order.[41]
This self-control is not to preclude enjoyment of life.

A joyful heart cheers the face,
and by sorrow the spirit is broken.
(Prov 15:13; see 17:22)

However, the key to the enjoyment of life's pleasures is moderation (Sir 31:19). Wine, for example, is a great good - within limits.

What is life to a man without wine?
From the beginning it was made for rejoicing.
Rejoicing of heart and gladness of soul
is wine drunk in season and temperately.
(Sir 31:27b-28)

If thoughts, action and will are devoted to the guidance given by wisdom,[42] then life will be enjoyable in a well ordered way.

Chapter I - Aphoristic Wisdom: Four Motifs

Both Kohelet and Jesus depart from the doctrine that self-control is the primary way to authentic life. Kohelet does not deny that self-control is often required in life's practical exigencies (see Koh 8:2-4 and the proverbial wisdom of Koh 10); this is in keeping with his position that practical wisdom is a necessity but that theoretical wisdom collapses before the reality of death. However, when it comes to experiencing satisfaction in one's existence it is necessary to abandon the effort to negotiate one's way in life by self-restraint in thought, word and deed, and to accept agreeable, happy feelings in the present. Kohelet therefore sets another dimension against that of disciplined thought and behavior, the dimension of immediate, pleasurable experience in eating, work and conjugal relations.

> Behold what I myself have seen: Good and fitting it is to eat, drink, and enjoy oneself in all the labor that one does under the sun all the days of the life that God has given him; for this is his portion (ḥeleq).
>
> (Koh 5:17)

Kohelet continues in saying that God answers man "in the joy of his heart" (5:19).

Jesus's aphoristic wisdom teachings include little or nothing about the virtues of silence and the need for moderation and balance.[43] He recognizes that there are affairs that require common sense and persistence (Matt 7:24/Lk 6:48; Mk 2:21 pars.; Matt 7:7-11/Lk 11:9-13). The human condition is one of care that imposes a certain level of anxiety which is expressed in foresight, prudence and shrewdness. But this anxiety defeats itself if it is not channeled by commitment to God's care (Matt 6:19-34). Jesus does not call the principle of self-control into question as much as he bypasses it. He envisions a new divine order arriving in the world, and this new reality imposes a demand that one commit oneself to it rather than preserving an old one. The aphoristic sayings of Jesus actually function as mediating insights between the old order and the new order. "Whoever loses his life for" (a higher or transcendent good) - this is ancient wisdom recognized by Jew and gentile alike.[44] "...For my sake and the gospel's" - this is the new announcement, the appropriate response to which is wholehearted commitment and joy, not self-restraint.

31

The kingdom of heaven is like treasure hidden in a field,
which a man found and covered up; then in his joy he
goes and sells all that he has and buys that field.

(Matt 13:44)

E. Aphoristic Wisdom of Order and Counter-Order

Now that the foregoing motifs have been presented we
move into the heart of the study. Presupposing the motifs as
references that structure and suggest significant material
and ideas, we shall proceed to examine ancient Jewish
aphoristic wisdom with respect to its form and content. The
study seeks an understanding of both conceptual and literary
aspects of gnomic wisdom; as already stated, it wants to
probe the relation of consciousness and knowledge to forms
of expression.

Order was the dominant underlying principle of the four
motifs presented. In our examination of traditional wisdom
on retribution, language, authority, and the self we
repeatedly confirmed a statement in the introduction to the
chapter: a concept of order is at the very center of wisdom
thinking. Yet we also discovered at every point that the
teachings of Kohelet and Jesus either denied the principle of
order or diverged from it in a significant fashion. This
divergence, broadly stated, was based either on an image of
the experimenting, celebrating self (Kohelet) as opposed to
the value of the disciplined self, or on affirming a joyous
self-surrender to God's new rule (Jesus) as against the worth
of the self centered in wordly care and prudence. These
positions fall roughly into perspectives of order and
counter-order. We shall therefore continue the study by
investigating the aphoristic wisdom tradition under these
two broad categories, the aphoristic wisdom of order
(Proverbs and Sirach, with Abot basically in the same
tradition) and the aphoristic wisdom of counter-order
(Kohelet and Jesus in the synoptic gospels).

Important issues began to emerge as expressions of the
fundamental tensions between order and counter-order.[45]
These may be delineated as the individual and the particular
versus the typical and the general; experience and novelty in
conflict with tradition; and the positive, representing
function of language as opposed to the negative, paradoxical
questioning of received ideas and images.

32

Chapter I - Aphoristic Wisdom: Four Motifs

(1) <u>The individual and the particular versus the typical and the general.</u> The gnomic form requires a generalization in order to arrive at a maxim or teaching of broad, perhaps universal validity, yet it is in principle based on individual experiences and particular situations. What are the function and authority of the individual person in relation to the prior and environing realities of tradition, society and nature?

(2) <u>Experience and novelty in conflict with tradition.</u> A given tradition is constituted by a multitude of symbols, stories, principles and ideas that have some sort of experiential base and that determine the individual's capacity to shape his experiences. Yet individuals have new experiences, and events perceived as hitherto unknown occur in the social and natural worlds. "Experience" is the engagement of a being which is "conscious" or "aware" with itself and other realities and beings.[46] Human being is that being conscious of its consciousness and able to assimilate experience through the symbolization and conceptualization of the various elements of experiences so that it can move further and further from predetermined patterns of instinct. Yet the patterns of tradition may become alienated from an individual's or group's drives, feelings, concerns and ideas. What is the status of experience, whether of a group or of an individual, in relation to the authority of the ongoing tradition?

(3) <u>The positive, representing function of language opposed to the negative, paradoxical questioning of received ideas and images.</u> We have already noted that language is not only a cultural given but the capacity to create symbols and ideas that constitute a human world. The positive function of metaphor is essential to this world-making, for it enables humans to bridge the distance between experiences and previous cultural facts to new symbols and ideas. It translates (Gk. metaphoros, "carrying over")[47] the unknown or the dimly perceived by the use of well known images.[48] The metaphor seeks "mimesis," to represent something that transcends the occasion and the subject speaking. Paradox, on the other hand, issues from a "dialectical" thinking that questions and relativizes accepted opinions and traditional knowledge. Paradox may be communicated through image and metaphor, but in this case the metaphor has a negative function vis-à-vis a

tradition, old order, or prevailing opinion. This negative function may express a thorough-going skepticism or it may be based on a vision of a new or transcendent order which stands against the status quo. If used constantly with deliberate intention paradox becomes a reminder that one can never quite achieve adequate representation, that the truth is always other than what the human standpoint can grasp. What are the forms and functions of paradox vis-à-vis the representing functions of language?

The basic issues will be explored in the following two chapters as we sketch the aphoristic perspectives of order and counter-order. We shall then bring the results of this study into conjunction with the interpretations of some contemporary literary critics in order to arrive at a literary-conceptual model of aphoristic discourse.

Chapter II

THE APHORISTIC WISDOM OF ORDER

A. Cases and the Typical

What are the function and authority of the individual person in relation to the prior and environing realities of tradition, society and nature? The aphoristic wisdom of order tends to view human existence and the environing world under rubrics of the general and the typical. However, the delineation of this view must be qualified by a consideration of the place of particularity, variety and mystery in gnomic thinking.

The aphoristic wisdom of order presents very few "cases" where the particulars of a situation are clearly pictured prior to generalization. Abot, for instance, is composed primarily of maxims. Since it was intended as a compendium whose object was to provide a summary of what the "fathers" (sages and rabbis) had taught, it does not disclose the particular matters that are found in the legal cases catalogued in the rest of the Mishna. The proverbs of the book of Proverbs deal with all sorts of topics. The collections of proverbs in Prov 10-29 could have served as "loci communes."[1] Usually, however, the cases of Proverbs are already represented in the form of the typical. Likewise in Sirach. Still, there are instances where the situation in its particularities is intimated (e.g., the toils of the rich man and the poor man, Sir 31:3-4). An example indicating even the thought process is Prov 24:30-34:

> 30. I passed by the field of the sluggard,
>   and by the vineyard of one lacking in sense.
> 31. And see, it was grown over with thistles,
>   nettles covered its surface,
>   and its stone wall broken down.

32.   And I looked, I took note,
       I saw, I learned a lesson.
33.   A little sleep, a little slumber,
       a little folding of the hands to lie down,
34.   and your poverty comes like a vagrant
       and your want like a beggar.

Here we see the process of observation (vv 30-31) and reflection (v 32), which leads to the conclusion expressed in proverbial form (vv 33-34). In this case the tension between the specific situation and the generalization is somewhat attenuated because the figure observed, the farmer-husbandman, is immediately identified as lazy.

The debate form in Sirach is unusual in that the specific questions or assertions of someone holding an opposing position are presented.[2]

Do not say, "Because of the Lord I have transgressed,"
for he will not do what he hates.
Do not say,[3] "He led me astray,"
for he has no need of violent men.

(Sir 15:11-12)

In addressing himself to the problems of skepticism and moral laxity in the hellenistic period Sirach tells us much about the specific setting as he perceives it.[4]

We find in the aphoristic wisdom of order that the individual and specific situations are important, but proverbial thinking is here inclined to search out the general and the typical in the individual and particular. As von Rad has said, for human beings of old it was the "breakthrough" (Durchstoss) to the general and the universally valid that was of greatest importance; it was, indeed, an elementary form of mastering complexities which enabled the knower of maxims to attain a certain "technique for life."[5] Yet the fact that certain things repeat themselves over and over again does not mean that one can draw up overarching patterns that encompass all phenomena of a certain sort. Gnomic wisdom is an investigative mode that proceeds empirically. Von Rad has said it well:

Wisdom explores (tastet...ab) the phenomenal world to determine its orders, but allows whatever it finds to stand completely in its particularity (Besonderheit) . It is easy to confront certain proverbs with others, which do not agree at all in content, and indeed, they occasionally contradict one another.[6]

So even if there are "orders" or "ways" to discern in experience, the patterns pulled out do not allow one always to predict one's approach to a given person or situation. On the one hand, there is sense in the world, there are "orders" to which one must attune oneself in humility and self-control. On the other hand, a great many situations and types of experience are part of reality and cannot be systematized. For example, one approaches a fool in different ways:

Answer not a fool according to his folly,
lest you also be like him.

(Prov 26:4)

Answer a fool according to his folly,
lest he be wise in his own eyes.

(Prov 26:5)

Poverty may be the result of laziness (Prov 10:4), but there are poor people who are upright and rich ones who are crooked (Prov 19:1; 28:6). Poverty may be the result of sloth (Prov 19:15), but nevertheless one should give to aid the needy (Prov 19:17). In fact, is it even good to be rich? It may be the result of diligence and prudence. Yet

Wise in his own eyes is the rich man,
and the discerning poor man sees him through.

(Prov 28:11)

In Sirach this balancing between the general and the particular, between generalizing and yet allowing individual situations to stand in their particularity, is raised to the level of rhetorical method and philosophical principle. He comments on many different topics on which he presents an alternate side of the same question. His style involves moving from one view of a subject to another. There are passages where he presents contradictions or ostensible contradictions without resolving them:

1:14-16	fear of Lord is beginning of wisdom/ fear of Lord is perfection of wisdom
10:18-19	(Gk. 10:19-20) human race worthy/ human race unworthy
20:1-2	not reproving is good/not reproving is bad

20:9-10   windfalls are profitable/
                 windfalls not profitable
40:1-11,18   existence is servitude/existence may be sweet

There are other passages in which Sirach views two sides of
an issue, but he makes distinctions that reduce or eliminate
any sense of contradiction (12:8-9; 25:16-26:1-3, 13-18;
31:1-7, 8-11; 31:28-29; 41:1, 2-4; 41:17-23; 42:1-8 [cf. 41:16;
4:20]).

Sirach's style of presenting opposing and different aspects
of a subject corresponds to the principle of oppositions that
is at the heart of his doctrine of theodicy (33:7-15; 42:24-25).
Like the ancient sages he recognizes the great variety that
creation is, and he tries to comprehend it by means of this
principle. God regulates everything in a fashion that forms a
grand harmony out of the tensions and conflicts of things
that oppose one another. The principle leads him to accord a
considerable importance to those phenomena considered evil
and painful. Great labor and heavy toil were created for
mankind, but life is sweet for the worker (40:1, 18).

All things are twofold, one opposite the other,
and he has made nothing incomplete.
One confirms the goodness of the other,
and who can have enough of beholding his glory?
(Sir 42:24-25)

The sages of the wisdom tradition clearly desire the
expression and establishment of order in individual lives that
are in harmony with family, society and tradition. This
desire for order issues in a quest for knowledge which is
manifest in the proverbs. Some proverbs establish a relation
between situations or events (Prov 10:26; 26:11), others posit
links between phenomena through the form of argument "a
minore ad maius" (Prov 15:11; Sir 10:30-31).[7] A daring step
was the drawing of analogies between putatively disparate
phenomena.

Heaven for height and earth for depth
and the mind of kings - who can search them out?
(Prov 25:3)

Cloud and wind, but no rain;
a man who boasts of a non-existent gift.
(Prov 25:14)

Besides the two affirmations made by the proverb, there is

here a "tertium comparationis": "...as the third and most important, there is something common to the two affirmations made by the sentence."[8]

At the furthest remove, i.e., the most metaphysical, in the gnomic discernment of order is the numerical saying, whose form is close to that of the riddle.[9] Indeed, here are two of these sayings that are remarkable in that the point of reference, the "control," is not known.

> These three are never satisfied,
> and four do not say, "Enough":
> Sheol, a barren womb,
> the earth unsatisfied with water,
> and fire that never says, "Enough!"
>
> (Prov 30:14-15)
>
> Three things are too wonderful for me,
> and four I do not understand:
> the way of the eagle in the sky,
> the way of the serpent on the rock,
> the way of the ship in the middle of the sea,
> and the way of a man with a young woman.
>
> (Prov 30:18-19)

"The common factor here is simply that [these phenomena] surpass comprehension."[10]

So ancient aphoristic wisdom is an attempt to master the complexities of experience, but reality is a plethora of beings and events that cannot be systematically comprehended. Analogies that enable one to find one's way may carry the mind toward an ever increasing mystery of things, but neither the world's secrets nor the divine reality can finally be comprehended (Prov 16:1, 9; 19:21; 20:24; 21:2; 21:30-31). The recognition of complex, manifold occasions of experience and the affirmation of mystery in some of the proverbs point to a profound dimension of the emphasis on order: the world in which we live is too multifaceted and puzzling to master. One can live with some confidence in the world for reality responds and is malleable, but the tangled circumstances and unpredictable events of the world are such that <u>disorder</u> is always a present threat.[11] There is a great anxiety before the menace of disorder as expressed in intemperate speech, sexual looseness, immoderate use of alcohol, or anything that would affect sobriety and modesty. To be "wise" is to be orderly, self-disciplined, and to be "foolish" is to be disorderly, undisciplined. The wise man controls his thoughts and fears God (Sir 21:11).

In conclusion, the aphoristic wisdom of order sees human existence and the environing world under rubrics of the general and the typical, but individuals and situations are allowed to stand in their particularity in that they are not linked and organized into a systematic set of abstractions. The cognitive mode is one that seeks always to move close to the pole of order, but there is a limited, though significant field of play for engagement with variety, contradictions, and elements of puzzle and mystery.

B. Tradition and Control

What is the status of experience, whether of a group or of an individual in relation to the function and authority of the ongoing tradition? The aphoristic wisdom of order is clearly inclined to affirm and support society and tradition rather than the individual and novelty. The key figure in this inclination is the "father" and the primary linguistic mode of the tradition is the proverb. The proverb, however, is the literary expression of a type of consciousness whose quest for order is modified by acceptance of experience as multifaceted and unsystematizable.

In the previous chapter we took note of the importance of the symbol of the fathers, whose experiences and observations, refined by reflection, are passed on to the present. The authority of the fathers is that of a human voice, but it is not an individual's; an individual, from this point of view, is only a representative of the human whole of the tradition. A person's life is too short and fragmentary to be a creative source of wisdom.[12] The praiseworthy individual is important in this perspective on the world, but even when the individual is the grammatical subject of a proverb it is a type, a generic form of a person that is represented. A "good man" and the "righteous man" (Prov 13:22), the "wise woman" (Prov 14:1) - these are types, not individuals.

The individual is thus called upon to observe, decide, assert himself, but only within the framework of tradition. His inner voice is to be that of the "father" and "mother."

Hear, my son, the instruction (mûsār) of your father,

and forsake not the teaching (tôrat) of your mother.
(Prov 1:8)

In Abot the chain of tradition assumes a special importance. God created the world by Torah and the Jewish man, above all the sage, sustains the world by meditating upon Torah and protecting it. The Torah must be "fenced" (Ab 1:1), i.e., studied, transmitted and distinguished from all other sources and works. The work of fencing is that of maintaining the tradition (massōret). The maintenance of the tradition is a matter of care and self-discipline. The sage must not err in teaching, "for error in teaching amounts to intentional sin" (zādôn: Ab 4:16). This theme of care in keeping the Torah is related to the ancient wisdom principle of maintaining proper order in one's personal life. One is obliged to keep the fathers' words in one's heart, control the mouth and tongue, observe the commandments, maintain discretion (Prov 4:21; 21:12; 19:16; 5:2).[13]

The tradition, then, is a reality embodied in the figure of the parent, who may in turn represent the leader, teacher, counselor, et al. The principle that the individual is to follow is obedience of the "father," that is, to heed the tradition. Eventually, when theological concerns became increasingly a part of wisdom thinking in the postexilic period, the fear of Yahweh was affirmed as the basic principle of wisdom.

The fear of Yahweh is the beginning of knowledge....
(Prov 1:7)
All wisdom comes from the Lord,
and is with him forever.
(Sir 1:1)
To fear the Lord is wisdom's full measure....
(Sir 1:14)

Thus the voice of wisdom may be human, but it is founded upon the principle of wisdom's origin in God.[14]

The proverb (Hebrew: māšāl) was intimately associated with the process of discovery and maintaining the tradition.[15] This is not articulated in our texts until the postexilic period, but it is evident in these later texts that gnomic discourse was considered the primary vehicle of wisdom. To become wise is "to grasp a proverb and a figure, words of the wise and riddles" (Prov 1:6). For Sirach the scribe (sōpēr), who is a man engaged full-time in learning

41

and reflection, is dedicated to seeking out the wisdom of the ancients; this vocation requires above all penetrating "the subtleties of parables" and searching out "the secrets of proverbs" (Sir 39:1-3). The one who is wise ponders a māšāl (Sir 3:29; Heb 3:27) and composes many of them (Sir 18:29). These contexts seem to indicate a connection between understanding and writing proverbs and the other qualities of the wise man: caution, guarding against sin (Sir 18:27), obedience and humility as the implied contrast to stubbornness and pride (Sir 3:26-28; Heb 3:24-26).

So we learn that the māšāl was a preëminent form of the words of the wise, which would lead to knowledge and understanding if one took them to heart and mind. Our sources do not inform us as to why the proverb served this function.[16] Whatever the philological theories about the origin and use of the word "māšāl," it was especially associated with thinking, knowing and instruction. We would offer two reasons for this association. One is that gnomic discourse offers a medium of language that represents what is believed to be timeless and universal.[17] It abstracts and generalizes from human experience, while taking the great variety of human concerns with great seriousness. The other reason is that the aphoristic form is appropriate to a view of reality that we find in Israel's wisdom, a view that sees life in the world as a plurality of occasions and types of persons and events. The phenomena encountered in experience are neither made to cohere in narrative nor systematized into a consistent whole, but allowed to remain in their differences and variety.

In short, in the aphoristic wisdom of order there is an overwhelming preference to affirm and undergird society and tradition rather than the individual and novelty. The point where the individual meets the tradition is in relationship with the "father,"[18] a figure which includes the parent but which is also a metaphor of several kinds of guide. The individual internalizes the voice of the fathers and obeys it by guarding himself against disorder (folly). The primary linguistic mode of the tradition is the proverb, which offers wisdom of timeless and universal insight while lending itself to the perspective that life in the world is multifaceted and unsystematizable. Thus even the desire for order was modified by the recognition of a pluralistic whole that could not be systematically explained nor fathomed at its profoundest level.

C. Representation and Negation of Paradox

What are the forms and functions of paradox vis-à-vis the representing function of language? We can say generally that the gnomic wisdom of order is fully aware of life's paradoxes. However, since it seeks to express and provide a confidence in order and language, it is not characterized by literary paradox.

It is necessary at the outset to distinguish between literary paradox and the literary indication of paradox. By the former is meant the use of words and images in such a way that the conclusion or meaning comes as unexpected to those holding prevailing opinions that the paradox presupposes. The literary indication of paradox is a reference to a paradox, in reality or in a fictional world. It may be artfully done, but the meaning of the language is not changed or negated.

The aphoristic wisdom of order contains many references to paradoxes of the human situation. In fact, the human situation itself is viewed as a paradox in some proverbs dealing with retribution and divine reality.

> Digger of a pit will fall in it;
> roller of a stone, it will roll back on him.
> (Prov 26:27)

> A man's mind minds his way
> and Yahweh steers his step.
> (Prov 16:9)

> From Yahweh are a man's steps,
> and a human being - how can he discern his way?
> (Prov 20:24)

Sirach frequently notes the paradoxes of human existence (Sir 41:1, 2), sometimes in a manner showing his interest in the psychology of the human condition (Sir 31:1-2; 40:1-7). The rabbis of Abot characteristically perceive the life of human being, above all of the Israelite, as paradoxical. A great name is an excellent thing, but one cannot seek it. One can choose one's way, but within the confines of providence. One can be a free person, but only as a slave of Torah (Ab 1:13; 3:19, 21).

The gnomic wisdom that remained close to experience, without metaphysical or theological reflection, observed many specific paradoxes in life.

There is one who disperses and yet gets richer,
and there is one whose miserliness leads only to want.
(Prov 11:24)

Before destruction is pride,
before stumbling a haughty spirit.
(Prov 16:18)

Bread of falsehood is sweet to a man,
but afterwards his mouth is filled with gravel.
(Prov 20:17)

The paradoxical situation of man is that he can <u>count on
paradoxes,</u> so to say. Even if one cannot finally grasp a
cosmic order and the divine way, the paradoxes of existence
are formulated in such a fashion that the paradoxical
becomes comprehensible, the unpredictable is to be
expected.

On the other hand, literary paradox is not common,
although there are a few striking instances. One is Prov
13:24:

Who spares the rod hates his son,
and who loves him lets him learn discipline.[19]

This is a true literary paradox in that it is a reversal of the
ordinary use of language, and it linguistically counters some
common opinion. Here "love" (sparing the rod) = "hate"
(leniency) and "hate" (severity in childrearing) = "love"
(discipline).[20] Other literary paradoxes include the trans-
formations occurring in these proverbs:

By patience is a ruler persuaded,
and soft speech (lāšôn rakkâ) breaks bone.
(Prov 25:15)

The mind of fools is in their mouth,
but the mind[21] of wise men is their mouth.
(Sir 21:26)

The first proverb converts the ordinary meaning of
"patience" and "soft speech" so that they mean "true power"
and "true strength." The second <u>seems</u> to assert that both
fools and wise men are "mouthy," but a second look
indicates the actual contrast: the fool's mind is controlled by
his hasty speaking, whereas the wise person's use of
language and capacity to think are perfectly integrated.

But the literary paradox as such is relatively rare in the

aphoristic wisdom of order. Paradoxes are encountered in the world, and the human situation itself may be viewed as a paradox. The gnomic discourse centered in the quest for order does not, however, try to disorient the hearer or call undue attention to the tenuousness of existence and the reality of death. Its goal is rather to form a sense of order and intelligibility in the one who seeks wisdom. Its analogies are mostly constructive, its positive images and metaphors abound. Its key metaphors[22] provide a picture of coherence in the world as presently known. Let us now consider these key metaphors.

There is no one metaphor that dominates Prov 10-29. One finds there various metaphors that express the need for wisdom in thought and conduct and that point to the retributive principle that informs the world. We have previously indicated that this principle has its focus in language (Chapter I, A). The words "tongue" and "mouth" occur as metaphors of language and the act of speaking with great frequency, and nouns such as "word" and "counsel" are of undoubted importance.

> Death and life are in the power of language,[23]
> and those who cherish it will eat of its fruit.
>
> (Prov 18:21)

In Prov 1-9 the dominant metaphor, attaining the status of a symbol,[24] is wisdom itself. In Sirach the two grand metaphors, both of which function as symbols, are wisdom and the priesthood. He identifies wisdom as the Torah (Sir 24:1-23), and he speaks of the enlightenment she brings by employing images of paradise and the first man (24:25-29). The high priest is to be honored (7:29-31) and the presumably contemporary high priest, Simon, is described in exultant lyrical similes ("like the morning star among the clouds"; "like roses in the days of the first fruits") (50:1-21). The symbols of Abot are Torah, Scripture and tradition. Torah is the divine wisdom and teaching, which is known both in Scripture and oral tradition. Scripture is the written expression of the divine voice ("as it is said" is the formula used in Abot for citing Scripture). Tradition is the transmission of oral Torah, the decisions and teachings that extend and protect the written Torah.

The retributive principle of justice to which the metaphors of Prov 10-29 point asserts that life makes sense because there is a connection of thinking, doing and result. On the other hand, human devices and projects, as already indicated, are limited by a transcendent justice that may bring one's thinking and doing to unforeseen results. The metaphors expressing this principle are a "bridge" of language from consciousness to environing reality and back again. If the crossing is not always pleasant due to life's paradoxes, it is still a link with reality and the basis of a human sense of order and coherence. The metaphors of wisdom, priesthood, Torah, Scripture and tradition which function as key symbols in Prov 1-9, Sirach and Abot go even further in that they mediate the divine reality to participants in the tradition.

The centrality of key metaphors in the aphoristic wisdom of order and the paucity of literary paradox is in keeping with the quest for order and positive knowledge that will sustain the world known by the tradition. Wayne Booth has pointed out that metaphor is fundamentally "additive": the metaphoric words do not need to be discounted, and the "metaphoric act" is synthetic, putting together "what had not been unified before."[25] Gerhard Neumann, in a similar vein, calls the metaphor the main figure of the "final reconcilability of what does not belong together."[26] On the other hand, the paradox issues from dialectic thinking, which may negate its own metaphors. The metaphor seeks "mimesis," to represent something that transcends the occasion and the subject speaking, but as employed in paradox the metaphor may pull one back with the reminder that one can never quite achieve adequate representation, that the truth is "elsewhere" or "nowhere" from the human standpoint,[27] at least in existence as presently known. It follows from this character of paradox that the gnomic wisdom of order could not be characterized by literary paradox, and would avoid it even more because it is so acutely aware of the paradoxes of life. It seeks to express and bring about orientation in the midst of possible disorientation. It affirms that the unexpected occurs, but it aims at a perspective whereby the wise person can make sense of it. The purpose of the proverbs of order is that the wise person

receive effective discipline,[28]
righteousness, justice, and uprightness.

(Prov 1:3)

Chapter III

APHORISTIC WISDOM OF COUNTER-ORDER

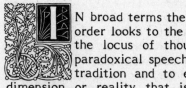N broad terms the aphoristic wisdom of counter-order looks to the individual's own experience as the locus of thought and value, and employs paradoxical speech to call into question a given tradition and to express the worth of another dimension or reality that is seen to stand against the traditional order. However, in keeping with this stress on the individual, the aphoristic wisdom of counter-order is more individualistic in its forms of thought and speech. Kohelet and Jesus cannot be characterized together except on a very general and broad basis. For this reason they will be considered separately in the ensuing chapter.

A. The Individual vs. the General

The individual has an important place in the teachings of Jesus and Kohelet. For Kohelet the individual, isolated from any sort of communion with God and the world, must heed and accept the possibilities given in the process of living when and where they emerge. For Jesus the individual's predicament is that of care and anxiety which, in his view, traditional wisdom simply compounds. The individual's hope lies in joyful acceptance of the imminent divine rule.

For Kohelet the source of wisdom, the limited wisdom that humans can obtain, is reflection upon the experiences of the individual. The way one should go and how one should know are to be "authored," so to say, by reflections bound to individual consciousness. The wise man and professional sage are not understood as individuals in the modern sense, for Kohelet's philosophy concedes the inexorable dominance of orders and types over individuals and specific events (Koh

1:9-22; 2:21). Nevertheless, the content of Kohelet's thinking and his literary style clearly give center stage to the voice of the experiencing self. His literary style is signaled in the formal organization of the work: there is a frame narrator who represents Kohelet (the "narrating 'I'"), who recounts his various experiments and experiences (the "experiencing 'I'").[1] The narrating "I" and the experiencing "I" cannot be considered apart, although the distinction is apparent when the speaker relates his life experiments (2:1, 12) and introduces his reflections with verbs of knowing and perceiving (4:1, 4, passim). The experiencing "I" is presented as a searcher, a seeker of wisdom (1:12, 13). He enjoyed pleasures of the flesh (2:1-3), engaged in extensive projects and acquired many possessions (2:4-11). He often feels that his labor is futile, but he sees that enjoying one's work is a great good (5:17). His quest, however, leads to negative conclusions about the possibilities of becoming truly wise.

The view of the subject that relates and ponders his experiences in life is that existence is like vapor; one cannot gain true profit, anything of lasting value, from existence.[2] Man is a being "divided" in a fateful fashion. Although everything that God does is fitting in its season, nevertheless God has placed "eternity" or what is "everlasting" (hā^{c}ōlām) in the human mind in such a manner that "man cannot grasp what God has done from beginning to end" (3:11). Man bears within his mind or self that which is at the very heart of the ongoing life that surrounds him and of which he is a part. This central reality is that which God does and has done, but human being is distant from a sense of real participation in it, and certainly has no control over it (see 1:15, 7:13). Man is entrapped between the secret of the divine reality implanted in his mind and the fleeting existence that is his lot and that prevents him from grasping this "^{c}ōlām."

In this predicament of being able to <u>conceive</u> of God, the everlasting, immortality, and true <u>wisdom</u>, yet of being caught up in a recurring round of things in which even man, with his mind, learning, and institutions, fades back into the cycle of that which appears and disappears, there is one recourse that Kohelet advocates: to enjoy that "portion" (ḥeleq) that may be found or received if one is fortunate enough to find it and is ready to accept it. This portion is a <u>happiness</u> which is the joy of the immediate experiences of work, eating and drinking, and conjugal love (2:10; 3:22; 5:17-18; 9:6, 9).[3] This happiness can be accepted, one may rejoice in it, but it may not be kept as "interest" or "profit" for the future. Kohelet's positive teaching therefore stresses feeling, the acceptance of agreeable and happy feelings in the present. The dimension of immediate, pleasurable experience is set in opposition to the order of thought and discipline transmitted in Israel's traditional wisdom.

> Behold what I have seen: it is good, indeed beautiful, to eat and to drink and to experience pleasure in all one's labor that one expends under the sun, all the days of the life God has given him, for this is his portion.... For let him remember that the days of his life are not many; for God answers in the joy of his heart.
>
> (Koh 5:17, 19)

So it is the individual that speaks in Kohelet (apart from the frame narrative, 1:1-2; 12:9-14), a self fully aware of individual selfhood and simultaneously believing that the individual belongs simply to the species of humankind. Like all instances of the generic and typical, the individual human appears and disappears without being remembered (1:10-11). Kohelet's is the voice of the individual confronting his own mortality, a condition which wisdom cannot heal or overcome. It is from this confrontation that the fundamental human paradox arises, that of mortal being that can reflect on its own mortality and yet know obscurely another reality, the everlasting, the work of God.

There is an ongoing life that God gives, there is that which endures, but it expresses itself in a tiresome round from the standpoint of the individual mind.

> All matters (hadd^{e}bārîm) are tiresome,
> One cannot utter (l^{e}dabbēr) it.
>
> (Koh 1:8)

There is a limited wisdom to attain; a wisdom that recognizes that God's world operates according to oppositions,[4] opposing seasons, the "right times" (3:1-8). Thus it is beneficial to see more than one side of a given problem and to have good judgment. But this wisdom is restricted, it will not lead one to the attainment of lasting value. "What profit is there for one in the labor that one expends?" (3:9) The polar structures of life cannot be affirmed as the marvelous order of God, as in Sirach, but are simply there to be accepted. From the standpoint of the mind existence is full of toil and trouble, and no symbolic construction can hide or overcome the fact of death. All one can do is to recognize the negative ("hēbel," no "yitrôn") and enjoy the immediate (heleq).

In the aphoristic wisdom of <u>Jesus</u> it is necessary to distinguish between the understanding of the individual in his message and his own self-understanding. The two would, of course, be closely related, but the figure of Jesus assumes such authority in the gospels and the history of Christianity that the distinction is an important one.

The individual is at the center of Jesus's aphoristic teachings. The individual may be depicted by means of types and caricatures, as in traditional wisdom, and in the church the individual was understood as one of the community of believers. But Jesus usually speaks of the individual in relation to his fellow humans, life's circumstances, and God. His words about the individual stress human care and the possibility of a change in one's situation. The locus classicus on human anxiety and the need to trust in divine guidance is the Q pericope, Matt, 6:25-34/Lk. 12: 22-31. There are two proverbs in this passage, Matt 6:25-26/Lk 12:22-23 and Matt 6:34. Both are in the ancient literary form of the māšāl. Luke 12:22-23 is an instruction māšāl:

Be not anxious for your life,
What you shall eat;
Nor for your body,
What you shall put on,
For[5] the life is more than food
And the body than clothing.

Human existence is rooted in life (psuchē) and body (sōma), but in seeking to secure life in the body humans tend to forget that experiencing this life is more important than the means of securing it. This counsel is completely different from the prudential advice of Prov 6:6-8:

Go to the ant, you sluggard!
Consider her ways and be wise,
Which without chief, overseer or ruler,
Provides her bread in the summer,
Gathers her harvest in the winter.

The individual should give himself over to God's care. There are affairs that require foresight, common sense and prudence,[6] but this anxiety defeats itself if it is not channeled by commitment of oneself to God's care. Of course, finding the right way that God ordains is not easy, it is narrow and difficult (Matt 7:13-14; cf. Lk, 13:24).[7] Perhaps most persons would prefer to have the best of both "worlds" or "spheres": survival (food, clothing, money, prestige, etc.) and life (God and his righteousness), but it is not possible to have a plurality of lords (kurioi); one's life must be centered in one master (Matt 6:24; Lk 16:13).[8] Yet even the servant who is faithful to his one lord must still exercise great care in the world, for his service takes place in the midst of great potential danger.

Behold, I send you out as sheep in the midst of wolves, so be wise as serpents and harmless as doves.
(Matt 10:16)

As a creature of care man is the object of God's care, and the one who accepts God's rule experiences the "kingdom" as the joy of discovering hidden treasure (Matt 13:44; cf. G Thom 109). It is like the satisfaction of locating a pearl of great price (Matt 13:45), like the gladness of a woman who finds a drachma that she has lost (Lk 15:8-10).

In short, Jesus views the anxious individual as paradoxically defeating his own ends: he loses what he most desires, "life," by seeking it in an anxious, self-centered way. The way out of this predicament is to give up one's "life" in the sense perpetrated by traditional wisdom[9] and to be committed to God's coming kingdom. The individual is typical in that he participates in a world of creatures and specifically in the human condition. However, his great possibility is to accept the divine care that raises him above subsumption in the generic round of things or the fate of death, for he is valued by God.

Are not two sparrows sold for a penny? And not one of them will fall to the ground without your Father's will. But even the hairs of your head are all numbered. So fear not, you are of more value than many sparrows.
(Matt 10:29-31; see Lk 12:6-7)

As for Jesus's self-understanding, how he viewed himself as an individual and bearer of a special office for God and man, this is a difficult subject, as already indicated. Jesus is presented often as speaking in the first person, and at times his authority is emphasized (e.g., Matt 5:21-48: "You have heard that it was said...but I say to you"). In other instances, and sometimes in the same pericope, he appeals to the authority of popular wisdom or Scripture. His authority is often grounded in an ancient collective wisdom.[10] The picture that emerges from the complexities of the texts is as follows. The new order, the rule of God, is discontinuous with the world preserved by God hitherto, yet this new rule cannot be understood apart from the law and the prophets and the wisdom that is "justified by her children" (Lk 7:35). The messenger, the one announcing this new order, was soon believed to embody it; perhaps he himself had this understanding. At any rate, this individual Jesus soon became for the early church the center of continuity and discontinuity with the Jewish tradition, the chosen one of God embodying the individual and the universal.[11]

In sum, Kohelet and Jesus both emphasize the authority of the individual experience in relation to traditional concepts of order. They both survey many life situations which they do not try to sum up in one overarching view. Kohelet believes that individuals are temporary, "vaporous" manifestations of recurring patterns and so are fated to be once more subsumed in the perpetual cycle of "the all" (Koh 1:2, 14). The divine way and doing is in man's mind, but it is for that reason so much the more frustrating that one cannot grasp it and comprehend it. One's positive expectation should therefore turn to the realm of immediate experiences, the very process of living. Jesus, however, images the individual over and over again as one able to find a great value. He is caught up in self-defeating care to maintain himself in the world, but his great hope lies in the word that he is indeed already valued by God the father. One must give up the maintenance of a little self-order as the primary concern and give oneself over to the new divine order, in which the meaning of the individual-in-community has everlasting significance.

B. New Experiences vs. Order and Tradition

Kohelet and Jesus both depart from the authority of tradition. Kohelet's authority stems from the observations and experiences of the individual, and he calls into question the traditional doctrine of self-control. He concludes that accepting one's portion in joy and pleasure is the key to a satisfying life. Jesus does not directly deny the doctrine of self-control but by-passes it in his vision of God's rule arriving in the world. This rule is to be received in great joy. Jesus's center of authority is different from Kohelet's for he claimed divine validation of his message. The church, in turn, moved toward faith in Jesus himself as divine.

The author of Kohelet certainly was informed by a tradition which gave him the material and point of departure that he shaped to the ends of his own thinking. He shows signs of familiarity with Genesis, Deuteronomy, and the deuteronomic history,[12] and he continuously cites proverbs that must have been well known. But the tradition that he knows is more of a foil for him than anything else; his use of gnomic forms, for example, is often in order to contradict traditional wisdom (see below, part C). There is a practical wisdom to be gained if one looks carefully to one's own observations and experiences, but the individual passing through the world is not significantly illumined and enlightened by the wisdom of the past. One may find in the latter some practical guidance in the face of political, social, and economic realities, but no light is shed on profound questions about God, the world, and mortality.

Kohelet's positive counsel is, in turn, very different from traditional wisdom. One should accept the gratification of physical and social desire rather than seek to be wise and productive through self-discipline. Kohelet advocates a certain moderation, which is very different from the traditional meaning of self-discipline.

> Don't be too virtuous (ṣaddîq) nor be too wise.
> Why destroy yourself?
> Don't be too wicked, nor be foolish.
> Why die before your time?

> (Koh 7:16-17)

Traditional wisdom amounts to "hēbel," vapor, in the face of human mortality and the human need to enjoy life while one still sees the light (11:7-8).

One of the signs of Kohelet's departure from traditional wisdom is the omission of a formula of address: there is only one occurrence of "bᵉnî," "my son," and it appears where the more conservative frame narrator speaks (12:12). The "fathers" as the symbol of the reality of the tradition has no meaning for Kohelet.

Of course, it is necessary to take into account the frame narrative in which Kohelet is identified as the son of David (1:1). The frame narrative pulls the book back into the tradition, so to say. It attaches Kohelet, albeit loosely, to Israel's sacral past and specifically to the authority of Solomon, the legendary king and sage. The recognition of this formal appeal to the authority of Solomon is important but it is only formal and is hardly resumed in 12:9-14.[13] We do not know how seriously the author intended this device of linking the speaker with Solomon. The strategy and contents of the work negate the value of traditional authority. The ironic result is that the great King Solomon is summoned (though not directly by name) to undergird the authority of the voice speaking on behalf of individual experiences and reflection.

The early Christian tradition knew <u>Jesus</u> as a teacher of aphoristic wisdom.[14] However, it is significant that many of the traditional wisdom topics are not found in the teachings of Jesus. There is little or nothing about seeking wisdom, building character, the virtue of silence, the seductive guiles of women, family relationships, human nature, government, and the need for moderation and balance.[15] The absence of admonitions to maintain "coolness" through silence, careful listening and avoiding the guiles of women is significant. In the aphoristic wisdom of order, self-control was based upon the principle of inherited order which was to be actualized anew in the life of the individual. We have seen how Kohelet called this principle into question, while Jesus bypasses it in envisioning a new divine order which is arriving.

Concerning the authority of Jesus vis-à-vis the tradition, the primitive church simply followed the pattern of Jesus's words and deeds in being oriented to the person of Jesus as the paradigm for interpreting the tradition. Jesus speaks as an authoritative voice in his own right. His speaking is different from Kohelet's because he claims a validation of his authority that is divine. Yet in speaking authoritatively, many of his sayings and stories were disorienting, calling traditional wisdom into question (see below, part C).

Jesus viewed himself as a prophetic voice and perhaps more, while the church - forgetting the obliqueness of parabolic speech and the inadequacy of metaphor - tended to identify him as the divine voice. In Jesus's understanding of his vocation the new order, the rule of God, is discontinuous with the world hitherto preserved by God; yet it cannot be understood apart from the law and the prophets, and the wisdom that is known from of old. (Matt 5:21-48 is a perfect illustration of this dynamic tension of continuity and discontinuity.) The messenger, the one announcing and embodying this new order, is the center, the transmitter and interpreter of this continuity and discontinuity. He speaks as the inspired "I" to individuals. The primitive church was both a community of believers and individuals who were each one addressed, so to speak, by their lord. The "I" of the lord addresses the personal center of each follower.

Why do you see the speck that is in your brother's eye...?
                              (Matt 7:3/Lk 6:41)
So if your eye is sound, your whole body is full of light....
                              (Matt 6:22/Lk 11:34)

For whoever should desire (thelē) to save his personal life (psuchēn)....
                              (Mk 8:35 pars.)

With this form of personal address from the "I" of Jesus to the personal center of the followers, the tension in the aphoristic form begins to break down as the speaker moves into exhortation and a call for commitment. The tension between general and particular and impersonal and personal, which in traditional wisdom was weighted more toward the general and impersonal, here becomes severely attenuated.

To conclude, the voice of Jesus is that of a human teacher quoting common human as well as scriptural wisdom, an eschatological prophet announcing the advent of God's reign and the arrival of the Son of man (unless Jesus identified himself with this title), and in the church's faith the very voice of God. This complexity involves a dialectical relation of tradition and novelty as the disciples interpret the tradition in light of the authority of Jesus's words and deeds.

EXCURSUS: The "Criterion of Dissimilarity"

In New Testament scholarship the so-called "criterion of dissimilarity," associated with the name of Bultmann,[16]

has had a great impact. This is especially so in the
hermeneutics that has been the basis of assessing the
influence of aphoristic wisdom in the gospels. Bultmann's
statement of the criterion is as follows:

> We can only count on possessing a genuine similitude of
> Jesus where, on the one hand, expression is given to the
> contrast between Jewish morality and piety and the
> distinctive eschatological character which char-
> acterized the preaching of Jesus; and where on the
> other hand, we find no specifically Christian
> features.[17]

The effect of this criterion is twofold: (1) it practically
eliminates any confidence we could have about the
ascription of the wisdom sayings (except the sharply
paradoxical ones) to Jesus, and (2) it prevents one from
seeing a dialectic of the eschatological and the
noneschatological elements in the message of Jesus.
Carlston's recent study of wisdom sayings in the synoptic
tradition infers that the church at every stage understood
Jesus as a teacher of wisdom whose teaching and preaching
were a dialectic of the eschatological and noneschatological, kingdom of God and timeless wisdom.[18]
The criterion of dissimilarity fits too easily into Christian
theological claims and the contemporary psychological and
sociological need to explain literary creativity as a mode of
religious expression. Dominic Crossan has travelled furthest
in the latter direction. When he asserts "that Jesus' use of
proverbs and parables is far closer to that of Zen Buddhism
than it is to conventional Hebrew wisdom" (In Parables: 77),
his argument is not wrong in what it affirms but in what it
denies. There is no question that Jesus used metaphors
expressing the paradox of God's rule in radically disorienting
ways. On the other hand, there is still much of traditional
Jewish wisdom in Jesus's teachings, both formally and
materially, even though many of the traditional wisdom
topics are not found in his teachings (see in this study pp.
22, 50-52 (and n. 9), 54, and 60-61). It appears to this writer
that Crossan's interpretation suffers from two errors: (1)
excessive dependence upon the questionable "criterion of
dissimilarity" (ibid., 5; see also Raid on the Art: 176) and (2)
an invocation of modern creators of anti-metaphor and
radical paradox which is sundered from any tension with

mimesis; this paradox is taken as the sole characteristic of Jesus's use of language (In Parables: 13; on Kafka see ibid.: xiv, and the treatment of Kafka and Borges in Raid on the Art).

We do not wish to gainsay that clear and unmistakable features of Christianity can be discerned in the gospels; but in some cases these traits are not so clear. And elements characteristic of Jewish thought, morality, and piety should be approached with special care, for even if Jesus differed from his Jewish contemporaries in some basic respects, much of what he said and how he said it would naturally have originated in his Jewish cultural and religious tradition. He stood at least as much within his tradition as outside of it.

C. Paradox against Life and Death

Kohelet and Jesus both employ literary paradox to disorient their audience. Kohelet's key metaphors are finally stilled in the paradox that negates traditional wisdom and points back to the joys of immediate experience as the source of good. The metaphors of Jesus serve paradoxes that nullify the present state of things, where man defeats his own ends, and prepare the hearer to heed the announcement of a new life.

To a point metaphor serves a positive function in Kohelet. Much of the book is sententious and as such is not cast in the language of poetic image and metaphor. Still, it may be held that Kohelet is a literary artist. His style and his images suit his thinking; his presentation is aesthetically appealing, as attested in Koh 12:10. One of the best examples of the integration of style, images, and ideas is the prologue on the cosmos and human existence, 1:3-11. The themes of repetition and vanity are extraordinarily haunting. To quote here only the first four verses.

> What is man's profit in all the labor
> of his work under the sun?
> A generation comes, a generation goes,
> and the earth always endures.
> The sun rises and the sun sets
> panting toward its place,
> where it rises (once more).
> The wind - it goes to the south,

and turns to the north,
turning, turning, goes the wind,
and on its circuit the wind returns.

(Koh 1:3-6)

The images and syntax evoke the sense of a monotonous cycle. Everything passes, comes back, but then it passes again like vapor or mist.

Likewise, the poem on old age (12:1-7) is a beautiful poetic expression of what it means to grow old. It concludes with the image of turning that is also so vividly expressed in the prologue:

And the dust returns to the earth as it was,
and the breath[19] returns to God who gave it.

(Koh 12:7)

Man exists between the earth that endures (1:4) and God. He is a passing reality composed of dust from the earth and breath ("spirit") given by God.

Kohelet uses certain images as metaphors of the human condition. Human existence is "hēbel," vapor, which issues in man's inability to achieve "yitrôn," a lasting advantage. A positive metaphor of human possibilities within the boundaries of a tenuous existence is "ḥeleq," "portion," denoting originally the portion of land that fell to a tribe or an individual by the casting of lots (see Josh 18:1-10; Mic 2:1-5). It took on the meaning of "inheritance," and in Kohelet man's "inheritance" is simply the joy of certain experiences if and when they occur. Another positive metaphor for Kohelet is light, which is associated with the sun and with seeing. Man's toil "under the sun" is a recurring refrain. The primary mode of cognition that he expresses in the formulaic introduction to his reflections is that of seeing (1:14; 2:3; 12, 13, 24, passim).

The wise man, his eyes are in his head,
but the fool walks in darkness.

(Koh 2:14)

Old age is a process of becoming darkened and blind, whereas youth is to "walk in the light of your eyes" (11:9).

And sweet is the light,
and pleasant for the eyes to see the sun.

(Koh 11:7)

Light thus represents the reality of everything pleasant in human experience.

Nevertheless, Kohelet views the human situation as paradoxical in its very depths (3:11). Even though it is better to be wise and "see" as compared to the fool's "darkness," yet "I myself perceived that one fate meets them both" (2:14). Human mortality and human ignorance of ultimate wisdom reduce the power of the positive metaphors of life. The human paradox of being entrapped between vapor and the reality of God's deeds, between dust and divine spirit is often indicated by Kohelet, but Kohelet also expresses it in literary form through the device of quoting traditional proverbs or his own aphorisms.[20] A few examples will be given.

At 4:5 Kohelet quotes what is evidently an old proverb (cf. Prov 6:10):

The fool folds his hands
and consumes his own flesh.

But the contrary is also true, according to another proverb (4:6):

Better a handful of repose
than two hands full of fatigue.

These contrasting proverbs illustrate Kohelet's contention that all exertion to compete and excel is "vapor and chasing after wind" (4:4b, 6b).

Another instance is 7:1. 7:1a has a simplicity of form and sentiment that probably identifies it as a popular proverb:[21]

Better fame than fine perfume.[22]

But 7:1b comes unexpectedly, and is as jarring as a zen koan:[23]

And the day of death than the day of birth.

Whatever be the interpretation of these two lines,[24] the rather conservative and traditional affirmation contained in the first proverb cannot have the same sense after having been joined to 7:1b. In fact, the seeming literary illogic of the joining of these two texts may have been Kohelet's method of indicating the absurdity of life: a good name amounts to little or nothing if the name's bearer must face the fickleness of fortune and a brief life span fading into death.

To give one more example, 9:4, the two sayings joined together there appear to express the worth of life, no matter how feeble or lowly it may be.

> For whoever is joined to all living has hope;
> for a live dog is better than a dead lion.

The affirmation in the first saying is known in many cultures.[25] It may seem surprising that he would say this given the thoughts in 4:2-3 and 7:1. Of course, an aphoristic thinker is not systematic and his words should be viewed as facets of ideas whose articulation varies with the many aspects of life-situations. However, we construe these proverbial sayings as subtle irony in this context, and as paradoxical in the sense that the language shifts to another, unexpected meaning when examined in context. The context is the topic of the inevitability of death (9:1-3, 5-6) and the exhortation to enjoy one's portion while one can (9:7-9), for the grave awaits (9:10). In this context, in which death is the framing subject, the two sayings amount to such a feeble affirmation of existence that the effect is to raise a question about its putative worth. It is like a back-handed compliment ("you look good for the condition you're in"). The hope or trust (biṭāḥôn) in 9:4a is commonly affirmed in the face of great adversity or grave illness.[26] And the living dog of 9:4b, even if better than a dead lion, is still the image of a lowly cur (I Sam 24:14: II Sam 3:8; 16:9) in comparison to a majestic beast!

In short, Kohelet subtracts from his positive metaphors of portion and light to the point that they are almost nullified. His primary literary mode of representing the paradox of the human situation is the citation of contrasting proverbs, some of which may be his own aphorisms, in order to contradict traditional wisdom.

Kohelet's key metaphors are either pessimistic concerning the values of existence or are negated and stilled in paradox. The metaphors of Jesus are overwhelmingly positive, and they characteristically serve paradoxes that nullify life in the present state of things for the sake of a life in a future, transcendent state of things.

The paradoxes of Jesus are often expressed in the form of antithesis. The antithetical aphorism is one of the common literary devices attributed to Jesus in the gospels.[27]

> The Sabbath was made for man and not man for the Sabbath.
>
> (Mk 2:27)

> For whoever would save his life will lose it; and whoever loses his life for my sake and the gospel's will save it.
>
> (Mk 8:35)

Both of these sayings are formulated as chiasms:

Sabbath ⟍⟋ man
man ⟋⟍ Sabbath

save ⟍⟋ lose
lose ⟋⟍ save

We find precisely this chiastic antithesis also in Lk 14:11 (cf. Matt 18:4; 23:12; Lk 18:14).

> For whoever exalts himself will be humbled,
> and he who humbles himself will be exalted.

Likewise in another Q passage:

> No one can serve two masters; for either he will hate the one and love the other, or he will be devoted to the one and despise the other.
>
> (Matt 6:24/Lk 16:13)

An instance of the chiastic antithesis of images in Matt 10:16 (cf. Lk 10:31). In the context of a missionary discourse, the second large collection of dominical teachings in Matthew, Jesus characterizes the disciples as innocents who must nevertheless be clever:

> Behold, I send you out as sheep among wolves; be therefore wise as serpents and harmless as doves.[28]

The images are of domestic, appealing animals vs. wild, dangerous animal

sheep ⟍⟋ wolves
serpents ⟋⟍ doves

Doves and sheep are associated with innocence and are offered in sacrifice. The wolf and the serpent are known as sly hunters.

An antithetical aphorism which breaks ordinary linguistic

expectations to the point of radical disorientation of the hearer is Mk 4:25 (Matt 13: 12/Lk 8:18/G Thom 41; see also Matt 25:29/Lk 19:26; G Thom 88):

> For to him who has will more be given; and from him who has not, even what he has[29] will be taken away.

This aphorism, comparable to a zen saying,[30] was modified in Luke ("even what he thinks that he has") and the gospel of Thomas ("even the little that he has"). These changes probably show the difficulty the tradition had in interpreting the puzzling paradox. The Marcan text may already explain a little bit: the person who loses out (in the kingdom) had "nothing" in the quotidian sense of "very little." Thomas makes this meaning explicit. Luke's version is the most significant departure from the other witnesses: the person who loses out only thought that he had something!

Jesus's use of paradox often topples into hyperbole. When this occurs the effect is comic. For example, there is the picture of the blind leading the blind (Lk 6:39; see Matt 15:14). This is an incongruity which is very funny or very sad, depending on one's standpoint and mood when one pictures it. There are religious leaders who have no sense of what to "swallow" and what to "strain out" as they engage in legalistic hypocrisy:

> You blind guides, straining out a gnat and swallowing a camel!
>
> (Matt 23:24)

There are those whose ability to see minute faults in others is astounding given the obstructions to their own vision (Matt 7:3/Lk 6:41). One of the most comic images is that of the rich man who is so "great" that he cannot squeeze through the small and narrow entrance to God's kingdom:

> It is easier for the camel to go through a needle's eye than for a rich man to enter God's kingdom.
>
> (Mk 10:25, pars.)

Both the aphoristic and the narrative parables of Jesus take away something from human life and offer something to it; they reverse expectations, yet encourage hope. Perhaps the only comparable modern master of metaphor and paradox in tension with each other was Kafka.[31] Yet Jesus is much more confident of his metaphors than is

Kafka. Kafka's "way" is simultaneously a "wavering."[32] Jesus's metaphor of the kingdom is made up of many rich and positive images, such as the joy of one who finds a precious pearl, or of one who comes upon a great treasure hidden in a field (Matt 13:44-46), or of a poor woman who finds her lost coins (Lk 15:8-9). If these images do not tell what the kingdom is (the "topos" or referent), they do more than express what it is not (the "atopos" or non-referent) in that they express how it is and comes to be among human beings.

The sayings and parables of Jesus are thus informed both by metaphors that represent a new life whose source is divine and metaphors that disorient the listener in questioning or undercutting expectations built up by traditional wisdom. It is a one-sided distortion to see only one of these sides of Jesus's use of language.[33] The tension of metaphor and paradox in the teaching of Jesus should not be read by means of a grid that turns it into a radical dichotomy of language and reality nor a fall into the darker side of paradox as in Kafka.

As we have seen, the church began at an early stage to interpret the Jewish tradition and the embryonic Christian tradition in the light of Jesus and his words. Thus it is that the literary topic of metaphor and paradox overlaps the theological subject of the person and office of Jesus, for even in the life and ministry of the historical Jesus he was coming to be viewed as the supreme metaphor and the supreme paradox of the divine reality in the world. The literary tension between the positive images of God and his kingdom and the paradoxical images of unexpected grace and power that impose upon the self-defeating quests of man are already intimated in the words ascribed to Jesus about himself:

But if I by the finger of God cast out demons, then the kingdom of God has come upon you.

(Lk 11:20)

Chapter IV

A LITERARY-CONCEPTUAL MODEL
OF APHORISTIC DISCOURSE

A. A Review of Results

The aphoristic wisdom of order and of counter-order clearly fall into different configurations in the issues treated: (1) The individual and the particular versus the typical and the general. (2) Experience and novelty in conflict with tradition. (3) The positive, representing function of language opposed to the paradoxical questioning of received ideas and images. Yet the two basic categories of aphoristic wisdom do not run in completely separate rivers with two different sources. They both are characterized by the māšāl and its derivative forms; gnomic discourse is thus a mode of literary expression and a vehicle of ideas. A wise answer is an occasion of joy, a timely word is pleasant! (Prov 15:23). The skeptic Kohelet shared with traditional sages the desire to integrate aesthetics and wisdom: "words of delight" and "words of truth" (Koh 12:10).[1]

The aphoristic wisdom of order and counter-order may diverge on the issues that we considered, yet there were points of overlapping and contact. Gnomic discourse lends itself to generalizations and maxims. As von Rad has said, "...for the ancients the breakthrough to the general and the universally valid was the most important thing."[2] And yet, gnomic discourse not only addresses itself to a plethora of life situations, but it may be employed for reflection on individual experiences (e.g., Koh 2:1-17) and combine a general truth with personal address that disrupts the impersonality of the maxim (e.g., Mk 8:35 pars.).[3] Of course, narrative forms may combine the general and the particular, but never quite in the same way as the aphoristic forms, which may pose abstract truths in poetic language or present maxims that are connected to personal reflections. Again we return to the fact that aphoristic discourse combines literary and conceptual features.[4]

Since aphoristic forms are associated so distinctly with the generalization involved in the statement of a maxim or principle, they are usual considered to be quite distant from the primary experiences that are constituted by perception, emotion, immediate relationships and intuition. Indeed, the gnomic wisdom of order tends toward keeping these primary experiences well under control (but see Chapter II, 36-37, 39-40). Yet a discourse characterized by proverbs and brief reflections served the author of Kohelet in his experientially based statement on the sadness and ephemeral quality of existence. Jesus, whose message was directed to the awareness and experience of a new order of things, was known as a speaker in parables (Matt 13:34/Mk 4:34).[5] Gnomic discourse, then, serves also those who seek to discover or stress an order of primary experiences against tradition and accepted doctrine.

Aphoristic forms would seem to be far removed from the poetic function of image and metaphor, especially when they are in the form of a general truth or a maxim.

> Treasures of wickedness do not profit,
> but righteousness delivers from death.
>
> (Prov 10:2)
>
> A good name is to be chosen rather than great riches,
> better than silver and gold is favor.
>
> (Prov 22:1)

There are images here that function metaphorically. "Treasures" means more than money, "death" is not simply the cessation of existence, "silver and gold" suggest worldly power as well as money and material wealth. Nonetheless, these images are subdued, and are subordinated to the dominant didactic thrust of the proverbs. But contrary instances meet us in which the rich and playful images dominate the proverb. The "soft tongue" that "breaks bone" (Prov 25:15) as a metaphor of wise persuasion, the fruit in the "hand of the tongue" as a metaphor of life and death (Prov 18:21), crippled legs dangling from the lame as analogous to a proverb uttered by a fool (Prov 26:7) - in these mᵉšālîm the image is an appealing and memorable entréee to understanding. In some proverbs the idea and the aesthetic properties are brought close together through a play on consonant sounds.[6] The antithesis of prudence and folly is tied in Prov 23:9 to two sets of consonants, b-z-n-y and k-s (ś)-l:

> In the ears of the witless (bᵉjoznê kᵉsîl) do not speak,
> for he will refuse the wisdom (yābûz lᵉśēkel)
> of your words.

The consonants of "fool" (kᵉsîl) and "prudence" (śēkel) are acrostics, as though the fool and the wise may look alike but really have a different arrangement of components! So also the phrases "in the ears of" and "he will refuse" are nearly acrostics, as if "hearing," associated with wisdom, becomes "refusal" (obstinance) in the fool.

The wisdom of counter-order does not use more metaphors than the wisdom of order; it tends rather toward metaphors that are used to express paradox.

> And the dust will return to the earth as it was,
> and the breath will return to God who gave it.
>
> (Koh 12:7)
>
> It [the kingdom of God] is like a grain of mustard seed, which, when sown upon the ground, is the smallest of all the seeds on the earth; yet when it is sown it grows up and becomes the greatest of all shrubs, and puts forth large branches, so that the birds of the air can make nests in its shade.
>
> (Mk 4:31-32)[7]

The verse from Kohelet is the conclusion of his poem on old age. The images of dust and breath (rûaḥ) are probably allusions to the myth of creation and paradise (see Gen 2:7; 3:19). "Dust" and "breath" are metaphors of the human life that God has given, but it returns (yāšûb) to its origin like everything that is (Koh 1:6-7). The parable of Jesus is not a narrative but an extended simile. Its structure is that of a simile proverb: God's rule is like a mustard seed - sown in the ground it is the smallest of seeds, grown up it is the greatest of shrubs. The paradox is obvious: somehow that which appears at first as small and insignificant becomes the "greatest" source of rest and shelter.

Often the paradox is so radical that metaphors are absent.

Preferable is fame to fine perfume,
and the day of death to the day of birth.
(Koh 7:1)
For to him who has will more be given; and to him who has
not even what he has will be taken away.
(Mk 4:25)

Kohelet's proverb is a sort of "anti-māšāl": the positive
assertion is negated in absurdity. The image of worldly
prestige and security is juxtaposed to the flat assertion that
the cessation of existence is better than its beginning. In
Jesus's paradox there is a slight modification of the
absurdity in the qualification "even" (kai), but it is the
picture of removing something from one who has nothing.
There are various ways to explain and remedy the absurdity
("who has not" means "who is poor," etc.), but they still
would not satisfy those who are concerned with the justice
of such an affirmation. What is clear is that the new reality
of which he speaks is contrary to human goals and
expectations.[8]

Thus what we find is not that gnomic discourse is devoid
of image and metaphor, but that it is made up of a broad
range of specific forms. At one end of the spectrum are the
principles and maxims that are either devoid of images, or
the images serve only to illustrate an assertion. At the other
end of the spectrum there are stark paradoxes that are
devoid of metaphor because they express or imply an
extreme doubt regarding the capacity of certain received
symbols and doctrines to represent reality. In the middle
range are the metaphors proper, often showing freshness,
richness and playfulness of expression and exhibiting basic
confidence in the reality to be represented.

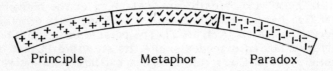

Principle   Metaphor   Paradox

In short, gnomic discourse is both poetic and
philosophical. It moves in a field of tension between the
general and the particular, reflection and situation, thought
and feeling. Its form and content may seem quite distant

from primary experiences, yet it is employed by those who, like Kohelet and Jesus in their respective fashions, are resolved to illumine and assert the rights of given dimensions of experience against received traditions and symbol systems. The literary form of aphoristic language may seem almost completely removed from the images and metaphors of poetic language, yet it also abounds in metaphor. In some instances, however, the paradoxes of aphoristic discourse become so extreme that metaphor, with its mimetic function, is practically absent. We shall now try to achieve a better theoretical understanding of this unusual combination of features by sketching a literary-conceptual model of aphoristic expression. To do this we shall first take into account recent literary critical studies of the aphorism. This survey of recent literary criticism will not be exhaustive, but it will provide a representative sample of modern literary interpretation of aphoristic discourse.

B. Aphoristic Discourse in Modern Literary Criticism

(1) Problem of Definition (see Excursus, p. 78)

Modern literary criticism has been little concerned with defining aphorism except in a very broad sense. One reason is that the history of short forms of speech in the Occident does not disclose compelling reasons to distinguish aphorism too discretely from other terms like proverb, sentence, gnome, maxim.[9] Dictionary definitions reflect common usage,[10] but they overlook certain features and they do not indicate that the aphorism has had a literary standing of sorts. H. U. Asemissen has sought to define the characteristic structure of the literary aphorism on the basis of its <u>effect</u> on the reader.[11] His definition, however, has not gained acceptance, in great part because it is too restrictive of those forms that are allowed as aphorisms. He himself was struck by the "small minority" of effective aphorisms.[12]

There is undoubtedly a consensus on general and basic features of aphoristic discourse. It is usually short and concise, and even when not short and concise[13] it is discourse made up of "units" or "elements" that can be separated out to stand in their own right. The biblical book of Kohelet is a "book" or a "work" and it contains various shorter and longer statements, some of them closely related in meaning to one another. But it is easy to lift out various speeches and many single sayings that do not require additional literary or historical context to be perceived by the audience as "complete." Finally, aphoristic discourse is peculiarly associated with effective speaking and thinking. Short forms are used for the sake of rhetoric and they are associated with a kind of practical thinking directed to specific life situations. It is also agreed that this is not a discursive or systematic type of thinking.

Beyond these points of agreement, however, there are widely diverging views. These disagreements concern the literary and philosophical status of aphoristic forms.

(2) A "Doctrine of Scattered Occasions"

Francis Bacon's proposals concerning aphoristic thought are well known in the tradition of aphoristic literature. His "doctrine of scattered occasions" (doctrinam de occasionibus sparsis), a phrase appearing in de Augmentis, means that aphoristic thought does not proceed systematically, but empirically. It directs itself to the fragments of experience as they occur, so that the mind is compelled to make its own connections among phenomena.[14] The influence of Bacon's doctrine is apparent in modern literary criticism.[15]

J. P. Stern has taken over Bacon's phrase for the subtitle of his important study of the great aphorist, Georg Christoff Lichtenberg (1742-99).[16] The subtitle indicates the influence of Bacon and humanistic scientific thought on Lichtenberg. As presented in Stern's exposition, the specific influence of Bacon on Lichtenberg had three features. (a) The aphorism is an empirical, antisystematic means of communicating certain ideas about nature. (b) The aphorism is appropriate for articulating moral precepts. (c) The aphorism, due to its pithiness and brevity, invites one to ponder hypothetical notions.[17] Here are three notes from Lichtenberg's Sudelbücher which illustrate, respectively, these three features.

> He made for himself a certain system, which had thereafter such an influence on his method of thinking that observers would see his judgment always preceding his perception (Empfindung), though he believed that it followed it. (D 485)

But it is presumption to believe that a being so mixed as man will acknowledge this all so PURELY [REIN - playing on Kant's Kritik der reinen Vernunft]. So that all the authentic wise man can do is to conduct everything to a good end, and still accept men as they are. (V 1012)

As a generally useful basis for lectures most manuals of physics are too detailed; they lack the requisite aphoristic brevity and precision of expression.[18]

The acceptance of Bacon's model of the aphorism continues without abatement.[19] There is, however, another aspect of Bacon's theory, one which has not had such a great impact in literature and criticism but which is nonetheless significant. This is the power of the aphorism to communicate the content of thought.[20] The aphorism, avers Bacon, eliminates illustration, examples, connecting links, and descriptions of actual practices. For this reason aphorisms are "the pith and heart of the sciences" because they are filled with nothing "but some good quantity of observations."[21] Bacon's view that the aphorism is a vehicle of thought is represented by many critics (Stern, Wehe, Requadt, inter alios).[22]

For Bacon this supposition meant that the aphorism functioned didactically, its language being only a <u>container</u> of truth. Yet this assumption flies in the face of another doctrine of modern critics, some of whom apparently accept Bacon's theory: the aphorism is a genre that consists in integration of form and content.[23] There is much at stake here. If form, apart from content, is the main attraction of the aphoristic mode of utterance, then "aphoristic thinking" would be a misnomer and aphorism could be approached only as literature. If content alone were its raison d'être, then it would function as moral philosophy, and probably poorly. If integration of form and content has been achieved in a full sense, then there have been and there are aphorists who have achieved a perfect, if fragmentary, linguistic expression and have overcome the ontic dichotomies of knower and known, thought and feeling, self and other.[24] This is a problem to which we shall turn in the subsequent discussion.

71

(3) Idea Paradises:
Gerhard Neumann on Post-Kantian Aphorists
Gerhard Neumann is a pioneering interpreter of aphorism
in modern German literature.[25] He is not concerned with
a precise definition of aphorism, holding that definition does
not lead to useful results. His argument is that the aphorism
has too indefinite a literary history to permit the
articulation of a genre.[26] If one thinks primarily in terms
of literary form, even recent self-conscious aphorists such
as Kraus, Valéry, Canetti and Lec have not held to any
identifiable set of stylistic conventions. For example:

The proximity of machine and organism in Leonardo is
the most sinister face of cultural history.... Its unrest is
that of the view that wants not to see what it
believes.[27]   (Canetti)

Who digs no grave for another falls in it himself.[28]
                                                          (Kraus)
Speak not evil of man. He sits within you and overhears
you.[29]   (Lec)

What is at the base (fond) of man? Some proverbs,
which end by responding to all, and are all ridiculous.
Deduction: profound (profondes) thoughts are not from
the depth (fond) of man but are prior to (avant) this
depth.[30]   (Valéry)

Neumann observes that there is an emerging consensus of
criticism in the use of "aphorism," but he notes also that in
fact there has been no real advance in defining a genre
beyond J. P. Stern's "paradoxical form" that entails a double
look at form and content.[31] There is an "unending
diversity of the individual expressions...."; between the
convergence upon the term aphorism and the variety of
texts "there can be no reconciliation, but only a constantly
vital interpolation, a critical argument between the
tendency to summarize and the tendency to note
particularities."[32]
What Neumann does in effect is to take aphorism into
account as literary genre, but to concentrate on its function
as a mode of thinking and knowing. His theory of aphoristic
thought and knowledge is oriented to the late 18th and early
19th centuries when a second "Copernican revolution"

occurred. The first one was Copernicus's theory that entailed saying to oneself, so to speak, "I feel the earth as fixed but I must think of it as moving." The second revolution, propelled above all by the philosophy of Kant, involved saying to oneself, as it were, "I know that I feel the earth as fixed and conceive it as moving around the sun, but I must think that this is a belief grounded in my capacity to reason and not in anything outside of this capacity." The result was a double dichotomy between thought and feeling. As Neumann has put it in summary form, "[man] perceives (erlebt) the sun as rising and thinks it as stationary, he experiences (erfährt) himself as subjected to the laws of nature and thinks of himself as lawgiver over against 'Nature.'"[33] The great German aphorists who experienced this new epistemological situation and responded critically to it - Lichtenberg, Novalis, Fr. Schlegel and Goethe - wanted to come to grips with it by developing a "transcendental ethics," a mode of approach to life and knowledge which would serve two functions: (1) enable humans to respond to opposing forces of experience and thought without losing either side of the oppositions; (2) establish the possibility of envisioning a new humankind, a new humanity not rooted in ancient mythology or eschatology but in a life of thought and imagination.[34] The aphorists did not seek to transcend or eliminate the poles of the dichotomies but to go through them by means of the aphorism.

> Man is perhaps half spirit and half matter, as the polyp is half plant and half animal. The oddest creatures are always on the boundary.
>
> (Lichtenberg, D 161)
>
> The opposition of body and spirit (Geist) is one of the most noteworthy and dangerous ones - great historical role of this opposition.
>
> (Novalis)[35]

"Thought becomes landscape"[36] - but aphoristic thought is not simply "utopian" for it directs itself simultaneously to the "topos," the situation of thinking and the object of thought. It issues from and gives form to the tensions experienced between body and mind, feeling and thought, representation and paradox, mimesis and utopia. Aphorism is an expression of the self that is both in internal dialogue and in conversation with others, both self-determined and seeing an objective design in reality.

Neumann refers all these tensions to the conflict between the "general" and the "particular." The aphoristic mode of expression has a remarkable place "between individual observation and general expression, between glancing at the particular and reflecting on a whole from which the particular receives its meaning, between 'detail' and 'system.'"[37] Generalizing is dangerous because one may thereby overlook or forget the individual who experiences and thinks in specific situations. So Canetti:

> The jump into the general is so dangerous that one must continually practice it, and from the same spot.[38]

But if it is dangerous, the aphorist believes himself obliged to do it for the sake of understanding, as in the case of Canetti who generalizes about the danger of generalizing.

The aphorism, then, originates in a particular situation, but it tends to generalize and form broad concepts. It seeks to plant seeds of thought while concentrating ideas in a short sentence or reflection. It is against systems of thought and politics which would subordinate individual experience to categories, but its generalizations and clever use of words rend it easily exploitable for systems. It represents the experiences and observations of a subject, but its frequently paradoxical form suggests more than a little suspicion of all objective knowledge. As a form of thought and knowledge, aphorism is simultaneously simple and complex. As Karl Kraus has said,

> One cannot dictate an aphorism into a typewriter. It would take too long.[39]

> An aphorism need not be true, but it should surpass the truth. It must pass over it (über sie hinauskommen) in one leap (Satz).[40]

To reiterate, Neumann views the aphorism as a mode of thinking and knowing which emerged from the great turning point of modern western cultural history. The basic conflict is between the particular[41] and the general, which is the "thoroughly effective principle of tensions (Spannungsgesetz) under which 'aphoristic' texts stand."[42] To aphoristic thinkers a "paradise of living" and a "paradise of ideas" seem neither to exclude each other nor unifiable without contradiction.

> The aphorism does not in this sense "lament" the contradiction between living and thinking, nor does it seek to abolish it. It undertakes rather to develop a form of knowledge out of the conflict of the two which makes use of reciprocal relatavizing of "representational" as well as "cognitive" ("logischer") means. This is a form of knowledge which builds a mistrust of the means of human knowing into every act of cognition and employs it for critical understanding.[43]

(4) The Dual Structure of Aphoristic Discourse:
    R. H. Stephenson

Drawing for the most part on works gathered in the anthology edited by Neumann, Der Aphorismus, R. H. Stephenson argues against what he considers "the widespread use of an inappropriate and restrictive model of the literary aphorism."[44] Stephenson's conclusions from his survey of modern criticism:[45]

a. The "Baconian" model "stresses the aphorism's capacity to communicate a thought in such a way as to stimulate further thinking."

b. This model "is accepted and employed throughout the critical literature."

c. Acceptance of this view of aphorism entails the conclusion that the content (concept) communicated is separable from and more important than the language of the aphorism.

d. There is a logical contradiction between this view that subordinates language to content and the equally widespread position of those "who argue for the literary status of the genre - that form and content are inextricably linked."

e. What actually happens to the critic employing the Baconian model is that aesthetic concerns are deflected "into a preoccupation with the message conveyed and with language as the means of its conveyance."

There are two interrelated problems with the Baconian model: form - content relation and the communication of new ideas. To take up the latter first, Bacon stressed the importance of aphorism for communicating new ideas and observations. His frame of reference was science, where understandably the knowledge of a previous generation of scientists would be new to their successors. But in the transmission of aphorisms we often find old ideas restated in new forms. One of Stephenson's examples is this maxim of La Rochefoucauld:

> However men may flatter themselves about their great deeds, these are not often from a grand design but from the effects of chance.

Stephenson comments that the notion that "pure chance, rather than design, is at the root of human achievement, hardly strikes one as an original thought."[46] He proposes that Logan Pearsall Smith is right in characterizing the aphorist as one who is concerned with commonplaces, and he suggests that the model of rhetoric appropriate to the aphorism is epideictic.[47] C. Perelmann and L. Olbrechts-Tyteca have drawn attention to this kind of rhetoric, which focuses on subjects "which are common knowledge and devoid of current interest."[48] As a literary model epideictic rhetoric would serve simply to account for the kind of discourse that seeks to please or delight the reader rather than to instruct or persuade him.

However, even if the aphorism is characteristically a "commonplace," it still has conceptual content. In some aphorisms the commonplace, extractable from the language, may seem banal; but the concept that is a commonplace may be so integrated into the texture of the language that the force of the idea is felt. What Stephenson proposes is that the literary aphorism must have a dual structure, two modes of literary organization which are distinguishable but inseparable. One of these serves to communicate a thought and one to wed the thought to an aesthetic form. The example he uses is one of Goethe's aphorisms:[49]

> Man sagt zwischen zwei entgegengesetzten Meinungen liege die Wahrheit mitten inne. Keineswegs! Das Problem liegt dazwischen, das Unschaubare, das ewig tätige Leben in Ruhe gedacht. (Hecker ed., no. 616)

> They say that the truth may lie between two opposing opinions. Not at all! The problem lies between that which is invisible, the ever active life contemplated in peace.

This maxim is not nearly as concise as it could be: it begins
as the quotation of a proverbial saying and the second line is
expansive. It thus lacks the brevity and conciseness of the
Baconian model, nor is it full of pungency. It begins
laboriously and uncertainly ("man sagt" followed by the
subjunctive verb "liege"). "Wahrheit" in this tentative
context sounds pretentious and complacent, whereas
"Problem" in the second sentence is given precedence by its
position and the sharper assertion involved in the indicative
phrase. However, the maxim does have linguistic features
which show why it may appeal to the reader. There are
consonant clusters in the first sentence that are tongue
twisting and the syntax is awkward; both of these problems
are straightened out in the second sentence where the
consonants run smoothly and the syntax is "straight-
forward."[50] Finally, the linguistic features have a dual
structure or a double mode of organization. There are two
thoughts juxtaposed in antithesis (a "fallacious" view and a
"correct" opinion). These conceptual relations are
coordinated with the linguistic texture. The syntax of the
"truth" is a problem and the syntax of the "problem" moves
forward easily. The consonants of the "false" opinion are
hurdles to get over and those of the "true" one flow. "....The
conceptual distinction becomes a felt difference."[51]

We have treated this double mode of linguistic organization in another context,[52] though the terminology
was different from Stephenson's. Let Prov 18:21 serve as the
example:

> Death and life are in the power of the tongue,
> and her friends will eat of her fruit.

That an idea can be extracted from this sentence is
evidenced by the various translations, most of which focus
on the idea of cultivating the proper use of language,[53]
which may bring life or death. The idea seems to be clear,
but it is wedded to sound patterns and striking images in the
Hebrew. The "tongue" - "language," with special stress on
the act of speaking - is a feminine noun, and "she" has fruit
in her "hand." This fruit brings life or death to her "friends."
The word for friend, "'ōhēb," means also "lover." The image
of the lovers of language is reminiscent of the adherents of
"ḥokmâ," Dame Wisdom (see Prov 8:17, 21; cf. 8:36). Since
the pronominal suffix ("her lovers") is feminine and "death"

and "life" are both masculine nouns, the possessive pronoun refers to the tongue: her lovers will eat of her fruit. The image of the feminine figure offering fatal or vital fruit to her lover(s) plucks the chord of a paradise myth and moves the death and life of the concept to a deeper level, the level of mythic metaphor. It is possible that even the consonants of the proverb participate in this poetic mode, as the labial sounds associated with the mouth and lips dominate the stichs (five in the first and three in the second). Here is a transliteration with the labials in upper case characters:

MāWet WᵉhayyîM Bᵉyad lāšôn
WᵉɩōhᵃBehā yōʼkal Piryāh

But what is the import of showing that aphorisms may be both literary and conceptual, with extractable ideas yet a coordination of rhetorical and morphological features? Is it not true that different forms of drama and poetry may be both poetic and philosophical? And are there not works of philosophy that are poetic (e.g., Plato's Republic, Nietzsche's Thus Spake Zarathustra)? The answer to these questions is yes, but the aphoristic mode of discourse has nonetheless a special place, a special role between extended discursive thought and the immediacy of feeling, between the experience of a particular situation and abstraction from many situations, between the individual that thinks and feels and the whole to which he belongs. The gnomic form is either still close to feelings and occasions of experience or, if it is a highly abstract maxim, it can still be at the disposal of the individual who hears it and reads it. It can appeal to or suggest myth and ancient symbol systems, but it does not require entering into them. It can offer signals of meaning and direction without coercing one's perceptions into the dictates of a system.

EXCURSUS: Aphorism and Proverb

Contemporary biblical scholarship has not concerned itself with clarifying the terms "proverb" and "aphorism."[54] This terminological confusion is understandable in that the history of the word "aphorism" does not indicate clear distinctions in usage.[55] If one examines the uses of the word "proverb," it also admits of great ambiguity. B. J. Whiting, for instance has shown that the Greek conception of proverb, "paroimia," was by no means clear.[56] He reconstructs Aristotle's understanding of "paroimia," which he employed more or less synonymously with "gnōmē," maxim. The resulting definition:

> A short saying of a philosophic nature, of great antiquity, the product of the masses rather than of the classes, constantly applicable, and appealing because it bears a semblance of universal truth.[57]

The one feature of this definition that most interpreters consistently associate with proverb rather than with aphorism is the proverb's popular origin. The same may be said of Whiting's own definition, which includes the phrase "owing its birth to the people."[58] This should perhaps be qualified to read "appears to owe its birth to the people"[59] (see below). Holman is in basic agreement with what Whiting says, although he highlights different aspects of the basic categories: "Aphorism implies specific authorship..." and proverb "has been preserved by oral tradition..."[60] Aphorism is thus more associated with a specific author and a literary tradition. Nevertheless, proverbs begin with individual authors or speakers.[61] Some current proverbs can be traced to known persons,[62] whereas we no longer have the historical information required to determine the origin of many ancient sayings.

These considerations are important, but not decisive. Proverbs may stem from one person no longer known. And although an oral tradition and popular appeal are characteristic of proverbs, what if we have speakers, like Kohelet and Jesus, who make sententious statements that often seem highly original, or some cases that read like proverbs but which may be original, deliberately archaizing formulations?[63] Whiting has presented a scholar's answer to this problem:

> A proverb...must bear the sign of antiquity, and, since such signs may be counterfeited by a clever literary man, it should be attested in different places at different times.[64]

This requirement, Whiting recognizes, cannot be met in ancient literature where we have incomplete material at our disposal. And Whiting's understanding is insufficient with respect to the proverb's origin: "folk authorship" is not a very useful concept.

Our viewpoint is that it is not helpful to distinguish proverb and aphorism too sharply in formal terms. The real difference between them is not so much formal as it is a matter of purpose and function. What was the intended use, and does the saying in question pretend to speak for a populace or tradition, or for an individual? The attribution of specific authorship to aphorism, and of popular origins and appeal to proverb are useful but not decisive characteristics.

What is decisive, in this writer's view, is the difference in principle between a <u>collective</u> voice and an <u>individual</u> voice. Both proverb and aphorism may employ metaphor. Proverb may be more associated with "homespun" language, but it can be quite clever and sophisticated.[65] Both are non-narrative forms that reveal and conceal a tension between the general (truth, principle, concept) and the particular (case, experience of subject), each seems to provide and evoke insight, and both may be paradoxical, although aphorism in modern western history is more associated with paradox and irony. What really distinguishes the two, if and when the distinction is valid, is their function, a function that does not always show itself in formal literary signs. The proverb expresses the voice of the human subject as ancient, collective wisdom, whereas aphorism (certainly the modern literary aphorism) brings the subjectivity of the individual more to the fore. But both accord a significant role to the human origin of the word spoken, whatever the ultimate grounding or authority of the utterance.

C. A Literary-Conceptual Model of Aphorism

What may we infer and extract from this survey of biblical aphoristic wisdom and modern literary criticism that will enable us to sketch a literary-conceptual model of aphoristic forms? Three dimensions of the problem emerge clearly for us: (1) Aphoristic wisdom is centered in a distinctive way in the concern with questions of order, disorder, and counter-order. (2) Aphoristic forms tend to polarize, either as vehicles to transmit and reaffirm a received tradition or to question accepted doctrines and opinions. In the case of the former the authority resides in a collective voice of the past, whereas the latter is centered in a given individual as authoritative or "oracular." (3) Aphoristic discourse has been both a literary mode and a means of communicating thought in the ancient world and the modern West. The dialectic of the general and the particular is an especially illuminating way of seeing the conceptual - cognitive side of aphorism, and the tension between metaphor and paradox is a fruitful fashion of viewing the poetic aspect of aphorism. These dimensions will be taken up in order.

(1) Order, Disorder, Counter-order

The aphoristic mode in a traditional society that seeks to conserve ancient values is a means of articulating timeless and universal types of values and behavior patterns (see Chapter II, pp. 36, 40). The proverbs of the book of Proverbs seek to mark out boundaries against death and chaos, which threaten ever anew if the individual does not heed the "parental" voices and maintain self-discipline. He who hears and obeys by acting in accordance with the ancient human voice of the ancestors will "profit":

> The treasures of wickedness do not profit,
> and righteousness delivers from death.
>
> (Prov 10:2)

Kohelet replied, of course, that there was no profit, there is no remainder that will protect one against disorder - the dissolution of death. In Kohelet's thinking one could be righteous (ṣaddîq) to excess (Koh 7:16), an impossible thought for Proverbs and Sirach.

But those who react against traditional wisdom's principle of order cannot advocate a principle of disorder. This would be completely self-contradictory and self-destructive. Their strategy may be one of disorder, that is, disorientation, but what they seek is another and better kind of order. What they pose against the timeless types of traditional order is an intuition or vision of a counter-order - a reality or dimension of reality that is over against the traditional or commonly accepted view of the world. For Kohelet this is the dimension of immediate experience where one may ironically receive and enjoy his "portion" in the very process of work, eating, and intimate human relations. For Jesus the counter-order is a transcendent state of things which is announced as God's arriving rule.

81

Modern aphorists have been known more as thinkers of a counter-order because they focus on the situation of the individual as his knowledge has been relativized to a degree that produces intellectual and spiritual vertigo. Still in all, the envisioning of another order, a better state of things, discloses a deep concern with the problem of order. Pascal, one of the modern pioneers of the aphorism as a mode of thought, shows this concern in a revealing fashion. He avers that the divine truth cannot be presented in rational or systematic order, for the latter participates in a fallen world. The method and mode of expression must therefore be a disorder that aims at disclosing the transcendent:

> I will write here my thoughts without order and not perhaps in a confusion without design. This is the true order, and it will always mark my goal by disorder itself. - I would honor my subject too much if I treated it in order, because I want to show that it is incapable of it. (P 532)

The proper "order" of treatment is the order of the heart, the order of love, which produces a strategy of digression:

> Order. Against the objection that Scripture has no order. - The heart has its own order, the mind (l'esprit) has its own which is by principle and demonstration.... J.C., St. Paul have the order of charity, not of the mind, for they wanted to humble, not to instruct. St. Augustine the same. This order consists principally of digression on each point which is related to the end [fin: God, Christ, salvation] so as always to show it. (P 298)

Later aphorists have adhered to a "transcendental ethics" rather than to a theology of the transcendent as Pascal, but they no less than he have sought to see and express the reality of an ultimate principle in human existence. It was Novalis who cried out,

> We seek the design (Entwurf) of the world - we are this design ourselves - What are we? personified omnipotent points.[66]

Even Kafka, the great master of paradox for whom meaning and value had receded into the inexplicable like Prometheus on the rock - even he was entranced by a vision of the "other side,"[67] and he could not shake off the thought of a

Chapter IV - A Literary-Conceptual Model

"true way" even as he nullified its meaning.

> There is a goal but no way (Weg);
> what we call the way is only wavering.[68]

> The true way (der wahre Weg) goes over a rope which is not stretched at any great height, but just above the ground. It seems more designed to cause stumbling than to be walked upon.[69]

One of the contemporary aphorists, Norman O. Brown, has employed the aphorism as an image of his own vision of a counter-order. Whereas systems are established as dominant orders, the true nature of human existence is a "broken body," love's body. The aphorism, as "fragment," is an expression of this broken body.[70] It represents death as part of the broken body and resurrection as the language of ecstasy or transcendent possibilities.[71]

> Aphorism is exaggeration, extravagant language; the road of excess which leads to the palace of wisdom.

> Aphorism, the form of the mad truth, the Dionysian form.

Brown's aphorisms are a remarkable "Dionysian" contrast to the "Apollonian" proverbs of the book of Proverbs. Yet he illustrates precisely the wide range of aphoristic thinkers on the spectrum of order and counter-order. He sees the aphorism as a linguistic form that expresses the "brokenness" of the present state of things. This condition is symbolized by the broken body of love, which is a double allusion: to the Christian myth of redemption and to the myth of Dionysius. The Greek god suggests the "madness" necessary to transcend a mad world, and the Christ intimates the fate of love in existence as known only through systems. Thus the aphoristic mode is a kind of linguistic disorder which enables one to leap into a vision of the counter-order of love that binds body and spirit together.[72]

In short, although aphorists may vary in their stance vis-à-vis a prevailing social order as they perceive it, they are characteristically concerned to articulate insights into an ideal forming of life, whether this be a principle of the order of creation, of primary experiences, of God's new domain, or of the world of thought and imagination.

Look upon all the works of the Most High: they likewise are pairs, one the opposite of the other.

(Sir 33:14-15)

The Pharisees asked him, "When will the kingdom of God come?" He said, "You cannot tell by observation when the kingdom of God comes. There will be no saying, 'Look, here it is!' or 'there it is!'; for lo, the kingdom of God is among you."[73]

(Lk 17:20-21) (Cf. G Thom 51; 113)

(2) Tradition and Skepticism

The role of aphoristic thinking in reinforcing a tradition or questioning a tradition is at one level the sociohistorical dimension of our study. That is to say, it is a question of the attitude toward the sources of authority and the agents who transmit wisdom through time. In this regard there is no doubt that the proverbial wisdom of ancient Israel was very conservative in its overt and implicit appeal to the "fathers." This appeal to the sages and elders does not reflect a sense of history in the modern sense; it is evident that the wisdom of the agents fades into a timeless past, a "time of origins," so to say. The individual and the present generation know nothing by comparison:

For enquire now of a generation before, and consider the experience of their fathers; for we are of yesterday and are ignorant, for our days are a shadow on the earth.

(Job 8:8-9)

The only way that Job could be wiser than the friends, who appeal to the mystery of God's way as well as to the wisdom of the ancients, would be if he had attained to wisdom in the very beginning of things:

Were you born the first of mankind?
Before the hills were you brought forth?

(Job 15:7)

Now when the skeptical Kohelet says nothing is really new (Koh 1:10), he is articulating a conviction of traditional aphoristic wisdom. He uses it, however, to draw a different conclusion, namely, persons and events are bound to repeat the past and be forgotten in the perpetual cycle of things. The wisdom of the ancients is either not remembered or it is ineffective.

84

There is no remembrance of former generations (ri'sōnîm), and also those that follow will not be remembered by those who follow them.

(Koh 1:11)

There is a conservative element in the teachings of Jesus insofar as he appealed to the law and the prophets, and generally to ancient wisdom ("wisdom is justified by all her children"). But this appeal to recognized sources of authority was in order to support his strong sense of personal destiny and authority as God's healer and messenger.

...Whoever loses his life for my sake and the gospel's will save it.

(Mk 8:35)

In all these instances save Kohelet there is a human voice whose wisdom transcends the immediate experiences of the individual. This human voice is the collective authority of the fathers in the aphoristic wisdom of order and the voice of the prophet-messenger in the sayings of Jesus (a voice that the church eventually acknowledged as divine). Kohelet's voice is the only one that justifies itself by reference to the good sense of the individual's reflections on his experiences. However, someone, probably the author himself, felt the need to use the fiction of Solomon's persona for the speaker in the book, and the frame-narrator uses a fatherly voice at the end to warn the inquirer against the excesses of books and study! The book Kohelet is thus enframed by the image of the legendary sage-king and the father who speaks with the voice of the past.

If we turn to modern aphorists, they are clearly great individualists who are preoccupied with the rights and possibilities of the individual.

Every man a finite God.
Each thing the entire world.

(Schlegel)[74]

The aphorists view man as the being who can imagine, think, and even live out of the transcendent; he bears a kind of immanent divinity which surpasses the individual. Consequently, although they stress the value of insights arising out of personal experience and do not appeal to

85

traditional sources of authority, the modern aphorists do not necessarily believe that the voice of their aphorisms is only their own personal word.

> Every man is only a part of himself.
> (Schlegel)[75]

> Appropriate here is what I have said in another context, that one should not say, I think, but it thinks, just as one says it flashes [es blitzt, there is lightning].
> (Lichtenberg, L 806)

> That (ce) which makes a work is not that one (celui) who places his name on it. That which makes a work does not have a name.[76]
> (Valéry)

In short, although aphoristic wisdom characteristically represents a human voice, it is simultaneously a voice that usually appeals to some sort of transpersonal, transhuman source of language and truth even if the aphorist is a skeptical and individualistic modern. The voice of the aphorist is a human voice that is at the same time another voice. Modern aphorists have frequently been troubled that this other voice is not representable through a tradition and a scripture that they could accept. This concern may account for the desire of some of the great German aphorists to gather their insights into a great book or encyclopedia of knowledge.

> This intended gigantic work [of Jean Paul] reminds one even to the details of the attempts of Lichtenberg, and especially of Hardenberg and Fr. Schlegel, to comprehend the most specific as well as the most general matters in a tremendous encyclopedia, a total novel, a Bible of aphorisms and groups of aphorisms. Aphorism and novel would be built into each other as the form of the conflict of human knowledge.[77]

(3) Aphoristic Discourse as Literary-Conceptual

It has been demonstrated, we hope, that aphoristic discourse maintains a peculiar tension of literary and conceptual elements; it is or may be both poetic and philosophical.[78] The cognitive side of this dual structure has not been explored by anyone in more depth and detail than Gerhard Neumann (see pp. 72-75). He points out repeatedly how the basic conflict in the conditions and contexts of human knowledge are brought together in the modern aphoristic tradition as a form and model of knowledge. The great aphorists have been unceasingly occupied with articulating and passing through the dialectic of the general and the particular, thought and feeling, reflection and situation, topia and utopia, representation and paradox.

The understanding of aphorism as both literary genre and conceptual vehicle has been advanced recently by R. H. Stephenson, although not as clearly as one could wish.[79] The interrelation of the two was recognized long before Kohelet's frame narrator affirmed that the sage intended his words to be both "pleasing" and "true." The artful proverb is a delight both in the realm of feeling and the sphere of thought (Prov 15:23). The editorial introduction to Proverbs avers that by studying and understanding these m^{e}sālîm the student will attain wisdom, instruction, discipline, and "skill" (taḥbulôt) to understand "proverb and dark saying (m^{e}lîṣâ), words of the wise and riddles" (Prov 1:6). Although the stress is here upon the didactic aspects of proverbs, the various expressions for the forms of gnomic language[80] indicate how closely associated certain forms of language and wisdom teaching were thought to be.

Since so much is concentrated in aphoristic discourse it is "charged," in the twofold sense of burdened and dynamized, with the tensions of thought and language. In the tendency to generalize, to abstract from many different feelings, thoughts and situations, there is a movement to overcome the transitory concreteness of specific things and persons. There is a drive toward representing pictures of order against the threat of disorder. But at times the feelings, thoughts and situations of given individuals and groups fall so far outside of the inherited, representable realities that the paradoxes always present in human experience - and recognized in traditional wisdom - begin to enter into the very language that seeks another set of insights into the order of things. Metaphor, which is indispensable to human being, thinking and speaking, and without which poetic language is impossible, begins to serve the power of paradox in the wisdom of counter-order.

The capacity to generalize is simultaneously the capacity of representation or mimesis; even if the representation is of a very specific reality, the representable reality fits into patterns that do not call knowledge and order into question. However, accident and death ("time and change," Koh 9:11) happen to everyone. If the individual cannot find his place in the representable patterns of reality, existence is a huge paradox: he has eternity in mind while his existence is vapor. Kohelet's way of responding to the claims of the experiencing individual against the language of the tradition from which he was alienated was to set proverbs against one another. Jesus, however, frequently concentrated both sides of the dialectical tensions in the same aphorism. Especially in the antithetical aphorisms do we find the various polar conflicts held together in striking tension. He engages in impersonal generalization ("whoever would save his life") vs. personal address ("for my sake"; "you cannot serve God and mammon"). He speaks of a loss of self which leads to gaining oneself (gaining "life" by "dying"). In general his strategy is one of representing the divine reality (kingdom of God, life) while using paradoxes that disorient the listener and imply that truth and healing are neither simply "here" and "there" as an object to consider (topia) nor "no-place" (utopia), but somewhere in between.

This concentration of polar tensions is literary, poetic and aesthetic, and philosophical, conceptual and logical. The dialectic of thought and feeling, of idea and image are held together in aphoristic discourse. Of the modern aphorists, none has done this more skilfully than Kafka. In fact, it has been argued that he sought to negate all metaphors to the point that the form itself - aphorism, parable, novel - becomes its own metaphor.[81] Be that as it may, he certainly used metaphor and logical reversal to surprise the reader[82] and elicit a deeply felt thinking of paradox.

As fast as a hand holds a stone. But it holds it fast only to throw it that much farther. But to just that distance extends the way.[83]

Here the hand that grips the stone grips it in order to let it loose, to throw it farther. But the evocation of thought lies mainly in the puzzling conclusion: the "way" (an important image for Kafka) is as far as one throws the stone.

The martyrs do not undervalue the body, they cause it to be elevated on the cross. In this they are at one with their opponents.[84]

The martyrs sacrifice body for spirit, but at the same time the "raising" of the body is what both they and their opponents want to do! The reader is induced to reflect on the double meaning of "auf dem Kreuz erhöhen," "elevate on the cross."

Grasp the good luck that the ground on which you stand cannot be greater than the two feet that cover it.[85]

This aphorism starts out in a vein alluding to the security of having one's feet firmly planted on the ground, but the good fortune turns out to be that the ground is just the area of one's two feet. A tenuous stance! Is the meaning that one's "ground" (Boden) is oneself (the grounding of "myself" has to be "my self")? The metaphor of paradox gives rise to thought, the paradoxical thought focuses attention on the metaphor.

* * * * * * *

What we propose, then, is that aphoristic discourse be understood as comprising nonnarrative modes of reflection and poetic expression that arise out of the deeply felt ontic tension between order and disorder and that are employed either to reaffirm a tradition or to articulate a counter-order which is based in experiences not validated by the tradition. These aphoristic modes are characterized by a twofold linguistic organization, literary and conceptual, poetic and philosophical. They are intended to illumine and stay close to the occasions of experience by a compact tension of the primary cognitive movement between the particular and the general and the primary aesthetic movement between representation and paradoxical questioning.

This model of aphoristic discourse offers three advantages. (1) It provides a broad but definite range of variations that enables the enquirer to see the similarities and differences between ancient proverb and modern aphorism and between ancient sage and modern aphorist. (2) It grounds a point of view that encourages literary critic, philosopher and theologian to investigate aphoristic biblical texts and to understand their work as interrelated. (3) It suggests a method of engaging in theological reflection that is opposed alike to systematic theology and to any "impressionistic" poeticizing or retelling of stories, for aphoristic discourse characteristically seeks to maintain both the "mental" and the "senuous" poles of human experience.

Order. Against the objection that Scripture has no order. The heart has its own order, the mind has its own which is by principle and demonstration ... [The order of Scripture] consists principally of digression on each point which is related to the end so as always to show it.

(Pascal, Pensée 298)

NOTES
BIBLIOGRAPHY
INDEXES

NOTES

NOTES TO PREFACE

1   K. Kraus, Beim Wort Genommen, ed. H. Fischer (München: Kösel, 1965): 57. All translations from foreign languages are the author's unless otherwise indicated.

2   RSV, following Gk.; Heb. 3:27: "The mind of the sage will comprehend (yābîn) proverbs of the wise."

3   In the numbering of the Pensées we shall follow the order established by L. Lafuma in Lafuma, ed., Pascal: Oeuvres Complètes (Paris: Editions de Seuil, 1963).

4   The edition of W. Promies will be followed: Georg Christoff Lichtenberg, Schriften und Briefe, I and II: Sudelbücher (München: Hanser, 1968, 1971).

5   Literary Criticism of the New Testament (Philadelphia: Fortress, 1970): 30.

6   There is a movement away from the "aphoristic" strategy also in Prov 1-9, although it is still not a treatise as is Wisdom. We shall make occasional references to Prov 1-9 and 30-31, but the main source of supporting texts will be chs. 10-29.

7   See D. J. Selby, Introduction to the New Testament (N.Y.: Macmillan, 1971): 494-96 and the citations in C. E. Carlston, "Proverbs, Maxims, and the Historical Jesus," JBL 99 (1980): 87-105.

8   There is no consensus concerning the date of Job in its final form. There are some American exegetes who date Job in the late preëxilic or early exilic period prior to the Second Isaiah (Pope, Terrien, Sanders; Pfeiffer earlier in the 20th century). Our opinion is that those who maintain a

postexilic date have a better case. See G. Fohrer, Das Buch Hiob, KAT 16 (Gütersloh: Gerd Mohn, 1963): 29-32.

9   Q = German "Quelle," "source," the hypothetical collection of Jesus's "logia" from which Matthew and Luke drew. The evidence for it is the many teachings attributed to Jesus which Matthew and Luke share, but which are not found in Mark.

10   From the "Anmerkungen" appended to Kraus, Beim Wort Genommen, where the editor says, "Der Titel dieses Buches wurde in Anlehnung an den Aphorismus gewählt: 'Weil ich den Gedanken beim Wort nehme, kommt er.' "

NOTES TO CHAPTER I

Ancient Aphoristic Wisdom of the Jews:
Four Motifs

1   See the etymology of motif/motive: "causing to move," Webster's Third New International Dictionary (Springfield, Mass.: Merridian, 1965): 1475.

2   See J. L. Crenshaw's introduction in Crenshaw, ed., Studies in Ancient Israelite Wisdom (N.Y.: Schocken, 1976): 27-33.

3   J. L. Crenshaw, "Questions, Dictons et Epreuves impossibles," in M. Gilbert, ed., La Sagesse de l'Ancien Testament (Gembloux, Belgium: Leeuwen Univ., 1979): 96-111; Jack T. Sanders, "Ben Sira's Ethics of Caution," HUCA 50 (1979): 73-106.

4   See W. McKane, Proverbs: A New Approach (Philadelphia: Westminster, 1970): 437 on "yād lᵉyād."

5   So von Rad, Wisdom in Israel (Nashville: Abingdon, 1972): 129-30.

6   The "sentence" or "sentence proverb" is an observation or assertion composed of two members or "stichoi" which are usually in synonymous or antithetical

parallelism to each other. The example given in the text is Prov 17:27.

7 The "instruction" or "instruction proverb" is a saying of two lines or more which is in the form of an imperative or prohibition. The example presented in the text is Prov 23:9.

8 An exception is the friends of Job in the book of Job who argue from his present state of suffering back to the transgressions they think he must have committed.

9 See J. G. Williams, "What Does It Profit A Man?: The Wisdom of Kohelet," in Crenshaw, SAIW: 375-89.

10 On "hēbel", "vapor," as a motif in Kohelet see A. G. Wright, "The Riddle of the Sphinx: The Structure of the Book of Qohelet," in Crenshaw, SAIW: 245-66.

11 "ḥeleq", "portion," occurs at 2:10, 21; 3:22; 5:17-18; 9:6, 9; 11:2. See Williams, "What Does It Profit": 384-86.

12 William A. Beardslee, "The Wisdom Tradition in the Synoptic Gospels," JAAR 35 (1967): 234.

13 J. G. Williams, "Deciphering the Unspoken: The Theophany of Job," HUCA 49 (1978): 59-72, esp. 70-72.

14 In Christianity the concept of retributive justice has continued at the folk level, as well as among church leaders and theologians to some extent. And retributive justice has been a principle of Judaism all along, although World War II and Auschwitz have shaken its hold on Jewish thinkers.

15 According to the occurrences listed in S. Mandelkern, Qônqôrdansiyâ LaTānāk (Tel Aviv: Schocken, 1962).

16 On 23:11 see McKane, Proverbs: 377-80.

17 See M. Hengel, Judaism and Hellenism I, tr. John Bowden (Philadelphia: Fortress, 1974): 131-53, esp. 138, 148-53.

18 J. L. Crenshaw, "The Problem of Theodicy in Sirach: On Human Bondage," JBL 94 (1975): 48-55. The passages are 5:1-6; 11:23-24; 15:11-12; 16:17. The debate form has three relatively fixed elements: (1) prohibition ('al-tō'mar); (2) quotation of the doubter; (3) response or repudiation introduced with "kî."

19   Von Rad, Wisdom: 253.

20   See the translation of the verse and comment in J. G. Williams, "The Power of Form: A Study of Biblical Proverbs," Semeia 17 (1980): 47.

21   On the translation see ibid.: 45-46.

22   "La Sagesse de la Femme," in Gilbert, Sagesse: 112-16.

23   Ibid.: 114

24   Gk (3:29): "will ponder a parable."

25   In "The Power of Form" we rendered, "prefer fame to fine perfume," in order to express the chiasm in English (ṭôb šēm miššemen ṭôb). But this breaks the form of the "better than" proverb.

26   W. A. Beardslee, "Saving One's Life By Losing It," JAAR 47 (1979): 60.

27   "Biblical Hermeneutics," Semeia 4 (1975): 114.

28   Wisdom: 94.

29   The father-teacher and son-student are more the subject in the proverbs of 10-22:16 and 25-29, but the father-teacher is presented as the speaker who addresses his son in 1-9 and 22:17-24:22.

30   But see McKane, Proverbs: 405-406.

31   Following the Hebrew text. Note that Sirach associates the wisdom of the ancients with both prophecies and proverbs, but he emphasizes the māšāl (Gk. "parabolē" and "paroimia," 39:1-3).

32   Archer Taylor, The Proverb (Cambridge: Harvard Univ., 1931): 34-43.

33   Du Sens: essais sémiotiques (Paris: Editions de Seuil, 1970): 313.

34   Michael Fox, "Frame-Narrative and Composition in the Book of Qohelet," HUCA 48 (1977): 91.

35   See Fox, ibid.: 85-86, n. 7.

36   Two qualifications of the last statement: (1) The

author of Kohelet does not conceive the individual in a modern sense, for his philosophy grants the inevitable dominance of orders and types over individuals and particular events (1:9-11; 2:21). (2) Besides the experiencing "I" as represented by the narrating "I," there is also the voice of the frame narrator who implies a qualified disapproval of Kohelet's teachings (12:11-12) and links him to the Solomonic tradition (1:1).

37   "Hoti errethē" clearly refers to Scripture. Cf. the rabbinic formula "šenne^jemar," "as it is said" (Abot 1:17, passim).

38   So G. Vermes has contended. But according to Fitzmeyer, the paraphrastic use of "bar ^jenāš(a^j)" in the sense of "I" and "me" is not attested before the period of late Aramaic, after 200 A.D. See the discussion and references in J. A. Fitzmeyer, S.J., "The Aramaic Language and the Study of the New Testament," JBL 99 (1980): 20-21.

39   Crenshaw, "Questions," in Gilbert, Sagesse: 101.

40   A More Fantastic Country: Introducing Biblical Literature (Englewood Cliffs, N.J.: Prentice-Hall 1978): 167.

41   Jack T. Sanders, "Ben Sira's Ethics of Caution," op. cit., argues that whereas Sirach's ethics of caution is rooted in the wisdom tradition, Sirach departs from older wisdom in his extreme emphasis on a good reputation and avoidance of shame as the main features of self control. "In the Jewish wisdom literature prior to Ben Sira, then, the complex of ideas expressed in his ethics of caution is present (albeit not collected emphatically in the way that is in Ben Sira), except that the motivation of name and shame is less important than life as a motivation" (90). Sanders concludes that Egyptian influence is more significant than Greek literature in Sirach's concern for a good name and a shameless life (103-106). Sanders is correct in pointing out Sirach's stress on name and shame, but this writer thinks that the theme is a variant expression of the quest to maintain self discipline, the tradition and social order, and so is scarcely a departure from the ancient tradition.

42   In Sirach wisdom is fundamentally a theological image and concept, for it is a divine gift (1:1, 14, passim). In Abot the life of self- control is to be yoked to Torah (3:6).

43   C. E. Carlston, "Proverbs": 94, 98.

44   See Beardslee, "Saving": 61-64.

45   The latter often assumed the form of disorientation (evoking a sense of disorder) in the strategy of Kohelet and Jesus, but their intention is the positive expression of another "dimension" or "order" of reality.

46   We would attribute "awareness" and thus the possibility of "experience" to any sentient being, though the latter's capacity to assimilate and learn therefrom may be extremely limited or practically nil.

47   In Webster's Third New: 1420, the etymology given is "transfer, change."

48   See W. C. Booth, A Rhetoric of Irony (Chicago: Univ. of Chicago, 1974), on the "additive" function of metaphor (22-24, 177). Cf. Gerhard Neumann, Ideenparadiese: Untersuchungen zur Aphoristik von Lichtenberg, Novalis, Friedrich Schlegel und Goethe (München: W. Fink, 1976): 760. Paradox is the "Leitfigur 'letzlicher Unvereinbarkeit des Zusammengehörigen'," and metaphor is the "Leitfigur 'letzlicher Vereinbarkeit des Unzusammengehörigen'."

NOTES TO CHAPTER II

The Aphoristic Wisdom of Order

1   See R. B. Y. Scott's classification of topics in Proverbs. Ecclesiastes, Anchor Bible 18 (Garden City, N.Y.: Doubleday, 1965): 130-31, 171, and his statement on p. 3: "Rather it is a source book of instructional materials for use in a school or in private study, for the cultivation of personal morality and practical wisdom." See also McKane, Proverbs: 10-22.

2   See ch. I, n. 18.

3   Gk.; Heb. pen tōʹmar, "lest you say."

4   See ch. I, n. 17.

5   OT Theology, I, tr. D. M. G. Stalker (N.Y.: Harper and Row, 1962): 420-21.

6   Theologie des Alten Testaments (München: Kaiser, 1957): 419 (my translation of the German). "Abtasten," which I have rendered "explore," means literally to "feel out," a felicitous expression in this context.

7   Heb. 10:29-30.

8   Von Rad, Wisdom: 119.

9   See ibid.: 122.

10   Ibid.: 123.

11   This is closely related to the fear of death in Proverbs. See J. L. Crenshaw, "The Shadow of Death in Qohelet," in J. G. Gammie, et al., eds., Israelite Wisdom (Missoula, Montana: Scholars, 1978): 211-13 and n. 44, p. 216. He says that death in Proverbs is the "bitterest foe," whereas Sirach's view is more complex.

12   See von Rad, Wisdom: 192.

13   The verb "šāmar," "keep, guard," is almost always employed in these proverbs advocating self control.

14   See Bruce Vawter, "Prov. 8:22: Wisdom and Creation," JBL 99 (1980): 205-16, esp. 214-16. Vawter argues that "yhwh qānānî rēʾšît darkô" of Prov 8:22 means that "Yahweh took possession of a wisdom that he then proceeded to utilize in his work of creation...," and that the word "rēʾšît" should be translated "principle" or "model" (215).

15   "Māšāl" is here employed according to its most common usage in the wisdom tradition, namely as the sentence or instruction of two stichs. In Tanak it has a wide range of connotations which may have in common the idea of "likeness." McKane prefers the root meaning of "model" (Proverbs: 24-32), but we find that the idea of likeness runs through all the occurrences.

16   See discussion and bibliography in Crenshaw, SAIW: 13-16.

17   Simon J. de Vries, "Observation on Quantitative and Qualitative Time in Wisdom and Apocalyptic," in Gammie, Israelite Wisdom, makes this very point and infers a

similarity of the functions of aphoristic language and cultic ritual (268-69). "...Both cultic and gnomic (= wisdom) discourse speak characteristically not about the existentially experienced, historical present but about an ideal present that constantly recurs within a particular pattern of conceptuality" (268). Greimas holds, in a related fashion, to the closely connected functions of proverb and myth, both of which seek to place their respective subjects outside of time. Myth does this by referring gods and heroes to the "archē," the beginning, and proverbs by referring its concepts to a timeless present. (Du Sens: 311, 313) See also Barbara Herrnstein Smith, On the Margins of Discourse (Chicago: Univ. of Chicago, 1978): 69-75 on "Saying and Sayings." Especially pertinent to this study is her remark on p. 73: "In saying what 'they' say [the proverb], the speaker disclaims responsibility for the utterance but does not wholly dissociate himself from either its general 'truth' or its applicability to the particular situation at hand."

[18]   "Mother" occurs often, but the father-son relation is the primary figure.

[19]   But see McKane, Proverbs : 457 on "šiḥᵃrô."

[20]   Note the chiastic construction:
        sparing - hating
        loving - imposing discipline.

[21]   Some Gk. texts read "in their mind," which would make of this proverb a simple antithetical parallelism: "The mind of fools is in their mouth/ but the mouth of the wise is in their mind."

[22]   Key metaphors are not chosen for the purpose of illustration, but function necessarily, as it were, for a given subject, text or tradition. They inform and ground the thinking that takes place. See J. Dominic Crossan, In Parables: The Challenge of the Historical Jesus (N.Y.: Harper and Row, 1973): 11-12.

[23]   Heb. bᵉyad lāšôn. See discussion of this verse in Williams, "Power of Form": 47, 53-54.

[24]   A metaphor is an image that provides an inference by means of implied analogy or likeness from the known to the less known or the unknown. E.g., "all flesh is grass" (Isa

40:6). Grass is the image that adds to knowledge about the meaning of flesh; in fact, it here gives its essential meaning as finitude in contrast to the everlasting divine word. "Symbol" as we use it here designates a metaphor that (1) attains such a status that it is believed to have power in its own right (e.g., the national flag as a symbol encompassing many metaphors of nationhood), and (2) is both abstract and concrete (e.g., "freedom" is an abstraction, but "nation under God" is a symbol that includes the abstract, yet has concrete reality in the people who feel and commit themselves to "nationhood"). A symbol is always a metaphor, a metaphor is not always a symbol. Concerning Wisdom in Prov 1-9, it is an abstraction in one sense, but it is also concrete insofar as it is associated with human beings who seek it and who are known as "wise."

25   Booth, Irony: 22-24, 177.

26   Ideenparadiese: 760.

27   See Neumann, ibid.: 759-70.

28   McKane, Proverbs: "effective instruction" (211, 263).

NOTES TO CHAPTER III

Aphoristic Wisdom of Counter-Order

1   Fox, "Frame-Narrative": 91.

2   See Williams, "What Does It Profit": 381-84.

3   At 2:21 and 11:2 it is not clear whether "heleq" means "profit" or "joy." "Joy" makes good sense in both verses.

4   See J. A. Loader, Polar Structures in the Book of Qohelet (Beihefte ZAW 152; Berlin: de Gruyter, 1979).

5   No motive conjunction in the Greek.

6   Matt 7:24/Lk 6:48; Mk 2:21 pars.; Matt 7:7-11/Lk 11:19-23.

7   See Carlston, "Proverbs": 102.

8   Carlston, ibid.: 101, n. 108.

9   The relation of Jesus as portrayed in the gospels to the wisdom tradition is well illustrated by a comparison of Matt 6:24 and Prov 27:1. The similarity of the wording and the warning against the attempt to control the future is outweighed by the great difference in the two. Prov 27:1 enjoins caution, whereas Jesus instructs not to be troubled by anxiety.

10   Matt 12:33-35/Lk 6:43-45; Matt 24:28/Lk 17:37; Matt 10:16/Lk 10:3; Matt 11:19/Lk 7:35. See also Mk 6:4 pars.

11   The radical expression of this development is the myth of incarnation in John.

12   Robert Gordis, Kohelet: The Man and His World (3rd ed.; N.Y.: Schocken, 1968): 32-36.

13   Although 12:9-10 could be understood as a description loosely in keeping with the legend of Solomon (cf. I K 4:29-34).

14   Carlston, "Proverbs": op. cit.

15   Ibid.: 91-99.

16   Rudolf Bultmann, The History of the Synoptic Tradition, tr. J. Marsh (N.Y.: Harper and Row, 1962): 205; see N. Perrin, Rediscovering the Teaching of Jesus (N.Y.: Harper and Row, 1976): 39-40; J. D. Crossan, Raid on the Articulate: Comic Eschatology in Jesus and Borges (N.Y.: Harper and Row, 1976): 176.

17   Bultmann, op. cit.

18   Carlston, "Proverbs": esp. 91, 102-105.

19   "Rûaḥ" could also be rendered "spirit," but Kohelet does not believe in an immortal soul or spirit (see 3:19-21). In 12:7 "rûaḥ" signifies the life, including the intellectual faculties, that God has given.

20   See R. Gordis "Quotations in Wisdom Literature," in Crenshaw, SAIW: 220-44, esp. 234-36.

21   So Gordis, Kohelet: 266 and R. B. Y. Scott, Prov. Eccles: 235.

22   On this translation see Williams, "The Power of Form": 46.

23   See William A. Beardslee, "Parable, Proverb and Koan," Semeia 12 (1978): 151-77.

24   See Gordis, Kohelet: 266-67.

25   Cf. the Latin "dum spiro spero," "while I breathe I hope."

26   See Gordis, Kohelet: 304.

27   See Robert C. Tannehill, The Sword of His Mouth (Missoula, Montana: Scholars, 1975): 88-101.

28   See Bultmann, History of Syn. Trad.: 107.

29   Crossan, In Parables: 177.

30   See Crossan, ibid.

31   See H. Politzer, Franz Kafka: Parable and Paradox, rev. ed. (Ithaca, N.Y.: Cornell Univ., 1966): 84-85. But note our reservations concerning Crossan's appeal to the artistry of Kafka as a touchstone for understanding the proverbs and parables of Jesus (pp. 56-57). Kafka may have sought an absence of metaphor in which the work itself would become the metaphor, representing nothing beyond itself. See B. Allemann, "Metaphor and Anti-Metaphor," in S. R. Hopper and D. L. Miller, eds., Interpretation: The Poetry of Meaning (N.Y.: Harcourt, Brace and World, 1967): 103-23. For Jesus, however, the relation of language to the tradition, the God of salvation-history, and human community was still positive and effective, though he believed that man in the present was caught in the predicament of anxiety and spiritual suicide as he sought to establish his existence in a world passing away. The result is that Jesus's metaphors have strong referents concerning present and imminent possibilities under God, but are radically paradoxical concerning the world of traditional wisdom as a source of value and hope.

32   "There is a goal but no way; what we call the way is only wavering". M. Brod, ed., Hochzeitsvorbereitungen auf dem Lande und andere Prosa aus dem Nachlass (N.Y.: Schocken, 1953): 42 (#26*).

33   E.g., Crossan's interpretation of the paradoxical aphorisms, which he says are to remind us "that making it all cohere is one of our more intriguing human endeavors and that God is often invoked to buttress the invented coherence" (Raid on the Art: 73). This much we can agree with, but he goes too far in asserting that "coherence is our invention...." (ibid.). As a reading of the parables of Jesus this becomes a distortion because it imposes a modern ontology of the dichotomy of language and reality upon the gospel text.

NOTES TO CHAPTER IV

Aphoristic Wisdom of Counter-Order

1   John Mark Thompson has attempted to elucidate the relation of the literary and conceptual elements of proverbs in his book, The Form and Function of Proverbs in Ancient Israel (The Hague: Mouton, 1974: 21-34. He describes the "form" of the ancient proverb as fundamentally poetic, the use of poetic devices being to influence or convince the hearer in the manner of poetry. The "function" of the proverb is philosophical, though not in the form of dispassionate or systematic speculation (21-31). Thompson's book is useful, but his analysis of form and function does not shed much light. For instance, one could just as readily reverse his argument and contend that the proverb's function is poetic, for as Thompson himself indicates, traditional societies have delighted in the aesthetic elements of proverbs, riddles, and word-play in general (26). On the other hand, the "form" may be seen as conceptual or logical - i.e., the patterns of expression may be formal features of thinking such as establishing likenesses and priorities, positing antitheses, indicating reasons, etc.

2   Theologie des Alten Testaments, I:418.

3   Beardslee has shown that the paradox of "saving" one's life by giving it for a higher reality or value (usually the welfare of the nation) was a universally known paradox

in the Graeco-Roman world (Beardslee, "Saving"). We would observe that Jesus's aphorism differs in (1) his use of the Jewish māšāl form and (2) the element of personal address and appeal which confronts the individual with a particular person and a specific demand. The literary form of chiastic antithesis is not found in the extra-biblical sayings cited by Beardslee and Carlston ("Proverbs"). The "antithetical aphorism" was a characteristic trait of Jesus's manner of speaking. See Tannehill, The Sword of His Mouth: 88-101.

4   This combination of literary and conceptual features explains why aphoristic discourse could serve thinkers and poets reacting against systems and ideologies and yet appear in ancient times to be "more positively related to what was emerging as systematic and discursive thought than is the case with a Nietzsche or a Norman O. Brown" (W. Beardslee, Literary Criticism of the New Testament: 31.) The gnomic mode is peculiarly conceptual and poetic in keeping with the dialectic of the general and the particular that it maintains. On the general and the particular, see the discussion of Neumann's work, below, p. 74.

5   It is important to observe that "parabolē" in the synoptics often means "saying," "proverb," or "lesson" rather than a narrative form. See Mk 4:30-32/Matt 13:31/Lk 13:18-19; Matt 15:14ff./Lk 6:39; Matt 24:32/Mk 13:28/Lk 21:29; Mk 7:17, referring to 7:14:-15.

6   See Williams, "Power of Form": 44-47.

7   On this parable see Crossan, In Parables: 45-51.

8   Another paradox is that the "meaning" of this aphorism may be the same as others such as "who would save his life will lose it" and "the first will be last and the last will be first."

9   See F. Schalk, "Das Wesen des französischen Aphorismus," in G. Neumann, ed., Der Aphorismus (Darmstadt: Wissenschaftliche Buchgesellschaft, 1976): 79. See also in Neumann, ibid.: F. Mautner, "Der Aphorismus als literarische Gattung": 23-46. Note also G. Rostrevor-Hamilton, "Aphorism, Maxim, Proverb," in Cassell's Encyclopedia of World Literature, rev. and enl. ed., ed. J. Brown, I:35-37, and G. Neumann, Ideenparadiese: 44-47.

10   See, e.g., Webster's New Collegiate Dictionary (Springfield, Mass.: Merrian, 1979): 52: 1.: a concise statement of principle 2.: a terse formulation of a truth or sentiment.

11   "Notizen über den Aphorismus," in Neumann, Aphorismus: 159-77.

12   Ibid.: 161.

13   E.g., "works" or "books" like the Zarathustra of Nietzsche and Brown's Love's Body.

14   This is knowledge achieved and communicated by aphorism - "scientia traduntur ... per Aphorismos..." See Bacon's full statement, quoted by P. Requadt, "Das aphoristische Denken," in Neumann, Aphorismus: 342.

15   See Neumann's introduction to Der Aphorismus: 6-7, and 13.

16   Lichtenberg: A Doctrine of Scattered Occasions (London: Thames and Hudson, 1963).

17   Stern: 105-106. See Stern's summary of Lichtenberg's "doctrine," pp. 272-76. Stern says that the doctrine is an "inverted Categorical Imperative" according to which each occasion is to be seen as a "law unto itself.... Each single experience, each idea, and each fact comes to us not as a symbol of a world whose universal law it exhibits or intimates, but as a discrete and self-contained part of a world whose laws are as many as its parts. What all these occasions have in common is this, that each forms a self-contained whole and thus represents 'paradigmatically,' and for a brief moment only, the asymptomatic totality of experience...." (274).

18   From Phys., Math. Schriften, quoted in Stern, Lichtenberg: 111.

19   W. Grenzmann calls Bacon the "theoretician and master teacher" of the aphorism as mode of thinking. "Probleme des Aphorismus," in Neumann, Der Aphorismus: 182-83.

20   For this and the following paragraph I am indebted to R. H. Stephenson, "On the Widespread Use of an

Inappropriate and Restrictive Model of the Literary Aphorism," MLR 75 (1980): 3-5. A subsequent subsection will be devoted to Stephenson's essay (pp. 75-78).

21   From The Collected Works of Francis Bacon, eds. Spedding, Ellis and Heath (London: 1857-74), III: 405, cited in Stephenson, "Widespread Use": 4.

22   See Requadt, "Das Aph. Denken": 269; W. Wehe, "Geist und Form des deutschen Aphorismus," in Neumann, Aphorismus: 131.

23   So Stern, Wehe, Mautner. See Stephenson, "Widespread Use": 4.

24   Modern aphorists have indeed sought their own transcendental utopias of thought and imagination. See the discussion of Neumann's work, pp. 72-75.

25   His major works on the aphorism that are to be utilized in this study have already been cited: Ideenparadiese and Der Aphorismus (the latter an anthology in which he has brought together important studies published between 1933 and 1973). He has also written Konfiguration: Studien zu Goethes "Toquato Tasso" (1965); Der Nachlass Arthur Schnitzlers (1969); Deutsche Epigramme (1969).

26   Ideenpar.: 11-38.

27   Quoted in ibid.: 764.

28   K. Kraus, Beim Wort Genommen: 57.

29   In Neumann, Ideenpar.: 39.

30   P. Valéry, Mauvaises Pensées et autres (Paris: Gallimard, 1942): 31.

31   See Stern's summary in Lichtenberg: 216-17: "The aphorism, we have found, is a strange and surprisingly complex configuration of words. Its charm hides in an antithesis, perfectly integrated, issuing from a double look at a word or an idea. It conceals its autobiographical source yet displays its process of generation. It is self-conscious, yet never exhibits its author's self-consciousness unmodified. It is something of an experiment in words and ideas, yet it commits aphorist and reader alike to an irretrievable occasion in experience. It uses ideas and

sentiments culled from all manner of experience, or again the findings of science, philosophy, literary theory, and any number of other inquiries, yet it defies all the systems to which they belong and all coherence wider than itself. It strikes us as both remarkably philosophical and remarkably literary. To one side of it loom empty puns, to the other fragmentary reflections. It and its definition involve us in a great many second thoughts about distinctions which common sense thought firmly established. And it gives one insight while suggesting many - indeed we find it difficult to tell how many, since it is always a little more than their occasion and a little less than their cause. In brief, it is the most paradoxical of genres. Defining a paradox as that formulation of a partial or ostensible contradiction which originates from a particular experience and in its effects elicits an abundant range of insights, we conclude that the aphorism is the <u>literary emblem of paradox</u>."

32   Ideenpar.: 38.

33   Ibid.: 827.

34   See in this century, Valéry, Mauv. Pensées: 8, 10.

35   Cited in Neumann, Ideenpar.: 265

36   Joubert, quoted in ibid.: 818.

37   Ibid.: 39.

38   Cited in ibid.

39   Beim Wort Genommen: 116.

40   Ibid.: 117. Note the probable wordplay: "Satz" means both "sentence" and "leap."

41   The German "Einzelne" permits an ambiguity of fluctuation between "particular" and "individual," whereas English must use different words.

42   Ideenpar.: 827.

43   Ibid.: 830. See also "Einleitung" to Der Aphorismus: 18.

44   See above, n. 20.

45   "Widespread Use": 9-10.

46   Ibid.: 11.

47   Ibid.: 13.

48   Perelman and Olbrechts-Tyteca, The New Rhetoric, cited in ibid.

49   Ibid.: 14.

50   Ibid.: 15.

51   Ibid.: 17.

52   "Power of Form" - Parts 2.2 and 3.1.

53   LXX: Death and life are in the hand of the tongue; and those who rule her (kratountes autēs) will eat her fruits.
      NEB: The tongue has power of life and death; make friends with it and enjoy its fruits.
      RSV: Death and life are in the power of the tongue, and those who love it will eat its fruits.
      JPS differs in presenting an implied warning against indulging in the tongue's power: Death and life are in the power of the tongue; And they that indulge in it shall eat the fruit thereof.

54   See the use of the words in Beardslee, "Saving": 58; J. L. Crenshaw, "Wisdom," in OT Form Criticism, ed., J. H. Hayes (San Antonio, Tex.: Trinity U., 1974): 231; Tannehill, Sword: 88-101.

55   See above, n. 9.

56   Whiting, "The Nature of the Proverb," Harvard Studies and Notes in Philology and Literature 14 (1930): 274ff.

57   Ibid.: 278.

58   "A proverb is an expression which, owing its birth to the people, testifies to its origin in form and phrase" (ibid.: 302).

59   On this point see Archer Taylor, The Proverb (Cambridge: Harvard U., 1931): 34ff. and A. J. Greimas, Du Sens: 311, 313.

60   C. Hugh Holman, A Handbook to Literature (rev. and enl. ed.; New York: Odyssey, 1960): entries on "aphorism" and "proverb."

61   Taylor, Proverb: 34-43.

62   See Taylor's examples, ibid. E.g.: "Knowledge is power" (Bacon); "To err is human, to forgive divine" (Pope); "A good death does honor to a whole life" (Petrarch).

63   See Greimas, Sens: 311, 313.

64   "Nature of the Proverb": 302.

65   For example, Koh 7:1a: "A good name is better than fine perfume" (Heb. ṭôb šēm miššemen ṭôb), which is a clever chiastic construction.

66   Quoted in Neumann, Ideenpar.: 778.

67   See the parable, "On Parables," in Gesammelte Schriften, 2nd ed., vol. 5, ed. M. Brod (N.Y.: Schocken, 1946): 85. English tr. in The Great Wall of China (N.Y.: Schocken, 1970): 150.

68   Hochzeitsvorbereitungen: 42 (#26*).

69   Ibid.: 39 (#1).

70   Love's Body (N.Y.: Vintage, 1966): 187-88.

71   Both of the following quotations are from ibid.: 187.

72   The method, if not the theology, is reminiscent of Pascal. See above, p. 82

73   The ambiguity of the Greek "entos humōn estin" provides a perfect ending to this part of the chapter. NEB has this note on its translation: Or "for in fact the kingdom of God is within you," or "for in fact the kingdom of God is within your grasp," or "for suddenly the kingdom of God will be among you."

74   Quoted in Neumann, Ideenpar.: 469.

75   Ibid.: 566.

76   Valéry, Mauv. Pensées: 36.

77   Neumann, Ideenpar.: 803.

78   Besides the authors already indicated see also M. Margolius, "Aphorismen und Ethik," in Neumann, Aphorismus 293-304; H. Kruger, Studien über den Aphorismus als philosophische Form (Frankfort am Main: Nest, 1957); C. P. Magill, "The Dark Sayings of the Wise:

Some Observations on Goethe's Maximen und Reflexionen," English Goethe Society Publications 36 (1966): 60-82; S. Ungar, "Parts and Holes: Heraclitus/Nietzsche/Blanchot," Sub-stance 14 (1976): 126-41.

79   The relation of "epideictic" rhetoric to a "form and content integration" is unclear in Stephenson's essay. See the discussion, pp. 75-78.

80   There are five in Prov 1:1-6: māšāl, ʾimrê bînâ, mᵉlîṣâ, dibrê ḥᵃkāmîm, hîdôt.

81   So Beda Alleman, "Metaphor and Antimetaphor": 113-14.

82   See S Sandbank, "Surprise Techniques in Kafka's Aphorisms," Orbis Litterarium 25 (1970): 261-74.

83   Hochzeitsvorbereitungen: 41 (#21).

84   Ibid.: 42 (#33*).

85   Ibid.: 41 (#24).

BIBLIOGRAPHY

Allemann, Beda
    "Metaphor and Anti-Metaphor," in S. R. Hopper and
    D. L. Miller, eds., Interpretation: The Poetry of
    Meaning (N.Y.: Harcourt, Brace and World, 1967):
    103-23.

Amsler, S.
    "La Sagesse de la Femme," in Gilbert, Sagesse (see
    Gilbert): 112-16.

Asemissen, H. U.
    "Notizen über den Aphorismus," in Neumann,
    Aphorismus (see Neumann): 159-76.

Bacon, Francis
    The Collected Works of Francis Bacon, ed. J.
    Spedding, R. L. Ellis, D. D. Heath, 4 vols. (London:
    1857-74).

Barley, N.
    "The 'Proverb' and Related Problems of Genre-
    Definition," Proverbium 23 (1974): 880-84.

Bascom, W. R.
    "Four Functions of Folklore," in A. Dundes, ed., The
    Study of Folklore (Englewood Cliffs, N.J.:
    Prentice-Hall, 1965): 279-98.

Beardslee, William A.
    "The Wisdom Tradition in the Synoptic Gospels,"
    JAAR 35 (1967): 231-40.

___.   "Uses of the Proverb in the Synoptic Gospels,"
    Interpretation 24 (1970): 61-73.

___.   Literary Criticism of the New Testament
    (Philadelphia: Fortress, 1970).

___.   "Parable, Proverb and Koan," Semeia 12 (1978):
    151-77.

___.   "Whitehead and Hermeneutic," JAAR 47 (1979):
    31-37.

____. "Saving One's Life by Losing It," JAAR 47 (1979): 57-72.

____. "Plutarch's Use of Proverbial Speech," Semeia 17 (1980): 101-12.

Booth, W. C.
   A Rhetoric of Irony (Chicago: Univ. of Chicago, 1974).

Brown, Norman O.
   Love's Body (N.Y.: Vintage, 1966).

Bultmann, Rudolf
   The History of the Synoptic Tradition, tr. J. Marsh (N.Y.: Harper and Row, 1963).

Carlston, C. E.
   "Proverbs, Maxims, and the Historical Jesus," JBL 99 (1980): 87-105.

Collins, J. J.
   "Proverbial Wisdom and the Yahwist Vision," Semeia 17 (1980): 1-17.

Crenshaw, James L.
   "The Problem of Theodicy in Sirach: On Human Bondage," JBL 94 (1975): 47-74.

____, ed. Studies in Ancient Israelite Wisdom (N.Y.: Schocken, 1976).

____. "The Shadow of Death in Qohelet," in Gammie, Is. Wisdom (see Gammie): 205-16.

____. "Questions, Dictons et Epreuves impossibles," in M. Gilbert, ed., Sagesse (see Gilbert): 96-111. (See also "Impossible Questions, Sayings and Tasks," Semeia 17 (1980): 19-34.

Crossan, J. Dominic
   In Parables: The Challenge of the Historical Jesus (N.Y.: Harper and Row, 1973).

____. Raid on the Articulate: Comic Eschatology in Jesus and Borges (N.Y.: Harper and Row, 1976).

Dewey, K. E.
   "Paroimiai in the Gospel of John," Semeia 17 (1980): 81-99.

Fitzmeyer, J. A., S.J.
   "The Aramaic Language and the Study of the New Testament," JBL 99 (1980): 5-21.

Fohrer, Georg
   Das Buch Hiob, KAT 16 (Gütersloh: Gerd Mohn, 1963).

Bibliography

Fox, Michael
"Frame-Narrative and Composition in the Book of
Qohelet," HUCA 48 (1977): 83-106.

Gammie, J. G., et al., eds.
Israelite Wisdom (Terrien Festschrift) (Missoula,
Montana: Scholars, 1978).

Gilbert, M., ed.
La Sagesse de l'Ancien Testament (Gembloux,
Belgium: Leeuwen Univ., 1979).

Gordis, Robert
Kohelet: The Man and His World, 3rd ed. (N.Y.:
Schocken, 1968).

____. "Quotations in Wisdom Literature," in Crenshaw,
SAIW (see Crenshaw): 220-44.

Greimas, A. J.
Du Sens: essais sémiotiques (Paris: Editions de Seuil,
1970).

Grenzmann, W.
"Probleme des Aphorismus," in Neumann, Aphorismus (see Neumann): 177-208.

Hayes, J. H., ed.
Old Testament Form Criticism (San Antonio, Tex.:
Trinity Univ., 1974).

Heidegger, M.
Aus der Erfahrung des Denkens, 2nd ed. (Pfullingen:
Neske, 1965).

Hengel, M.
Judaism and Hellenism, I, tr. J. Bowden
(Philadelphia: Fortress, 1974).

Herford, R. Travers, ed. and tr.
The Ethics of the Talmud: Sayings of the Fathers
(N.Y.: Schocken, 1962).

Holman, C. Hugh
"Aphorism" and "Proverb," A Handbook to Literature, rev. and enl. ed. (N.Y.: Odyssey, 1960).

Holt, C. D.
"Sir Austin and His Scrip: A New Approach to The
Ordeal of Richard Feverel," Journal of Narrative
Technique 4 (1974): 129-43.

Hopper, S. R.
"Kafka and Kierkegaard: The Function of Ambiguity," American Imago 35 (1979): 93-105.

____. "Literature: The Author in Search of His Anecdote,"

in Restless Adventure: Essays on Contemporary Expressions of Existentialism, ed. R. L. Shinn (N.Y.: Scribner's, 1968): 90-148.

Jolles, A.
Einfache Formen (Tübingen: Niemeyer, 1930).

Kafka, Franz
Gesammelte Schriften, 2nd ed., vol. 5, ed. M. Brod (N.Y.: Schocken, 1946).

___. Hochzeitsvorbereitungen auf dem Lande und andere Prosa aus dem Nachlass, ed. M. Brod (N.Y.: Schocken, 1953).

___. The Great Wall of China, tr. W. and E. Muir (N.Y.: Schocken, 1970).

Kierkegaard, S.
"Diapsalmata," in Either/Or, vol. I, tr. D. F. and M. Swenson (Garden City, N.Y.: Doubleday AB, 1959): 19-42.

Kraus, Karl
Beim Wort Genommen, ed. H. Fischer (München: Kösel, 1965).

Kronenberger, L.
The Last Word: Portraits of Fourteen Master Aphorists (N.Y.: Macmillan, 1972).

Kruger, H.
Studien über den Aphorismus als philosophische Form (Frankfort am Main: Nest, 1957).

Kuna, F.
"Rage for Verification: Kafka and Einstein," in F. Kuna, ed., On Kafka: Semi-Centenary Perspectives (N.Y.: Harper & Row, 1976): 83-111.

Lec, Stanislaw
Unkempt Thoughts, tr. J. Galazka (N.Y.: St. Martin's, 1965).

Lewis, C. S.
"Wit," in Studies in Words (Cambridge: Cambridge Univ., 1967): 86-110.

Lewis, P. E.
"The Discourse of the Maxim," Diacritics, Fall 1972: 41-48.

Lichtenberg, G. C.
Schriften und Briefe, I and II: Sudelbücher, ed. W. Promies (München: Hanser, 1968, 1971).

___. Aphorisms and Letters, tr. and ed. F. Mautner, H.

Hatfield (London: Cape, 1969).

Loader, J. A.
Polar Structures in Qohelet, BZAW 152 (Berlin: de Gruyter, 1979).

Magill, C. P.
"The Dark Sayings of the Wise: Some Observations on Goethe's Maximen und Reflexionen," English Goethe Society Publications 36 (1966): 60-82.

Margolius, M.
"Aphorismen und Ethik," in Neumann, Aphorismus (see Neumann): 293-304.

Mautner, F.
"Der Aphorismus als literarische Gattung," in Neumann, Aphorismus (see Neumann): 19-74.

McKane, William
Proverbs: A New Approach (Philadelphia: Westminster, London: SCM, 1970).
___. "Functions of Language and Objectives of Discourse according to Proverbs, 10-20," in Gilbert, Sagesse (see Gilbert).

Meleuc, S.
"Structure de la maxime," Langage 13 (1969): 69-99.

Mieder, W., ed.
Ergebnisse der Sprichwörterforschung (Frankfurt am Main and Las Vegas: Lang, 1978).

Morton, Donald
"Eccentric Sage: The Development of Form in the Poetry and Fiction of George Meredith," unpub. dissertation, Johns Hopkins, 1971.

Neumann, Gerhard
"Umkehrung und Ablenkung: Franz Kafkas 'gleitendes' Paradox," DVjs, Sonderheft: Literatur des 20. Jahrhunderts 42 (1968): 702-44.
___. Ideenparadiese: Untersuchungen zur Aphoristik von Lichtenberg, Novalis, Friedrich Schlegel und Goethe (München: W. Fink, 1976).
___, ed. Der Aphorismus: zur Geschichte, zu den Formen und Möglichkeiten einer literarischen Gattung (Darmstadt: Wissenschaftliche Buchgesellschaft, 1976).

Pagliaro, H. E.
"Paradox in the Aphorisms of La Rochefaucauld and Some Representative English Followers," PMLA 79 (1964): 42-50.

Pascal, Blaise
Pascal: Oeuvres Complètes, ed. L. Lafuma (Paris: Editions de Seuil, 1963).
Perrin, Norman
Rediscovering the Teaching of Jesus (N.Y.: Harper and Row, 1976).
Politzer, H.
Franz Kafka: Parable and Paradox, rev. ed. (Ithaca, N.Y.: Cornell Univ., 1966).
Prang, Helmut
Formgeschichte der Kunst (Stuttgart: Kohlhammer, 1968).
Rad, Gerhard von
Theologie des Alten Testaments, I (München, Kaiser, 1957).
___. Old Testament Theology, I, tr. D. M. G. Stalker (N.Y.: Harper and Row, 1962).
___. Wisdom in Israel (Nashville: Abingdon 1972).
Requadt, P.
"Das aphoristische Denken," in Neumann, Aphorismus (see Neumann): 331-77.
Ricoeur, Paul
"Biblical Hermeneutics," Semeia 4 (1975).
Rostrevor-Hamilton, G.
"Aphorism, Maxim, Proverb," in Cassell's Encyclopedia of World Literature, rev. and enl. ed.
Roth, W.
"On the Gnomic-Discursive Wisdom of Jesus Ben Sirach," Semeia 17 (1980): 59-79.
Rylaarsdam, J. C.
Revelation in Jewish Wisdom Literature (Chicago: Univ. of Chicago, 1946).
Sandbank, S.
"Surprise Techniques in Kafka's Aphorisms," Orbis Litterarium 25 (1970): 261-74.
Sanders, Jack T.
"Ben Sira's Ethics of Caution," HUCA 50 (1979): 73-106.
Schalk, F.
"Das Wesen des französischen Aphorismus," in Neumann, Aphorismus (see Neumann): 75-111.
Scott, R. B. Y.
Proverbs. Ecclesiastes, Anchor Bible 18 (Garden

City, N.Y.: Doubleday, 1965).

___. "Folk Proverbs of the Ancient Near East," in Crenshaw, SAIW (see Crenshaw): 417-26.

Selby, D. J.
Introduction to the New Testament (N.Y.: Macmillan, 1971).

Smith, Barbara Herrnstein
On the Margins of Discourse: The Relation of Literature to Language (Chicago: Univ. of Chicago, 1978).

Smith, Logan Pearsall
A Treasury of English Aphorisms (London: Constable, 1928).

Stephenson, R. H.
"On the Widespread Use of An Inappropriate and Restrictive Model of the Literary Aphorism," MLR 75 (1980): 1-17.

Stern, J. P.
Lichtenberg: A Doctrine of Scattered Occasions (London: Thames and Hudson, 1963).

Stierle, K.
"Pascals Reflexionen über den 'ordre' der Pensées," Poetica 4 (1971): 167-96.

Tannehill, Robert C.
The Sword of His Mouth: Forceful and Imaginative Language in Synoptic Sayings (Missoula, Montana: Scholars, 1975).

Taylor, Archer
The Proverb (Cambridge: Harvard Univ., 1931).

Thompson, John Mark
The Form and Function of Proverbs in Ancient Israel (The Hague: Mouton, 1974).

Thompson, L. L.
A More Fantastic Country: Introducing Biblical Literature (Englewood Cliffs, N.J.: Prentice-Hall, 1978).

Thorlby, A.
"Anti-Mimesis: Kafka and Wittgenstein," in F. Kuna, ed., On Kafka: Semi-Centenary Perspectives (N.Y.: Harper & Row, 1976): 59-82.

Ungar, S.
"Parts and Holes: Heraclitus/Nietzsche/Blanchot," Sub-stance 14 (1976): 126-41.

Valéry, Paul
    Mauvaises pensées et autres (Paris: Gallimard, 1942).
Vawter, Bruce
    "Prov. 8:22: Wisdom and Creation," JBL 99 (1980): 205-16.
Vries, Simon J. de
    "Observation on Quantitative and Qualitative Time in Wisdom and Apocalyptic," in Gammie, Is. Wisdom (see Gammie): 263-76.
Wahl, Jean
    "Kierkegaard and Kafka," in A. Flores, ed., The Kafka Problem (N.Y.: Gordian, 1975): 277-90.
Wehe, W.
    "Geist und Form des deutschen Aphorismus," in Neumann, Aphorismus (see Neumann): 130-43.
Whiting, B. J.
    "The Nature of the Proverb," Harvard Studies and Notes in Philology and Literature 14 (1930): 274-307.
    ___. "Some Current Meanings of 'Proverbial,'" Harvard Studies and Notes in Philology and Literature 16 (1934): 229-52.
Williams, James G.
    "What Does It Profit a Man?: The Wisdom of Kohelet," in Crenshaw, SAIW (see Crenshaw): 375-89.
    ___. "Deciphering the Unspoken: The Theophany of Job," HUCA 49 (1978): 59-72.
    ___. "The Power of Form: A Study of Biblical Proverbs," Semeia 17 (1980): 35-58.
Wright, A. G.
    "The Riddle of the Sphinx: The Structure of the Book of Qohelet," in Crenshaw, SAIW (see Crenshaw): 245-66.

INDEX OF TEXTUAL REFERENCES

INDEX OF MODERN AUTHORS

[Note: If an author is cited in more than two notes on the one page of the reference notes, passim is written in parenthesis after the page number.]